SMART MOM
RICH MOM

KIMBERLY PALMER

SMART MOM
RICH MOM

How to Build Wealth
While Raising a Family

AMACOM
AMERICAN MANAGEMENT ASSOCIATION
New York • Atlanta • Brussels • Chicago • Mexico City • San Francisco
Shanghai • Tokyo • Toronto • Washington, D.C.

This publication is designed to provide accurate and authoritative information in regard to the subject matter covered. It is sold with the understanding that the publisher is not engaged in rendering legal, accounting, or other professional service. If legal advice or other expert assistance is required, the services of a competent professional person should be sought.

Library of Congress Cataloging-in-Publication Data

Names: Palmer, Kimberly, author.
Title: Smart mom, rich mom : how to build wealth while raising a family / Kimberly Palmer.
Description: New York : American Management Association, 2016. | Includes bibliographical references and index.
Identifiers: LCCN 2015050487 (print) | LCCN 2016005190 (ebook) | ISBN 9780814436806 (pbk.) | ISBN 9780814436813 (ebook)
Subjects: LCSH: Women--Finance, Personal. | Working mothers--Finance, Personal. | Families--Economic aspects. | Work and family. | Career development.
Classification: LCC HG179 .P18862 2016 (print) | LCC HG179 (ebook) | DDC 332.024/010852--dc23
LC record available at http://lccn.loc.gov/2015050487

About AMA
American Management Association (www.amanet.org) is a world leader in talent development, advancing the skills of individuals to drive business success. Our mission is to support the goals of individuals and organizations through a complete range of products and services, including classroom and virtual seminars, webcasts, webinars, podcasts, conferences, corporate and government solutions, business books, and research. AMA's approach to improving performance combines experiential learning—learning through doing—with opportunities for ongoing professional growth at every step of one's career journey.

Dedicated to my amazing grandmothers, Janet Shearer Johnson and the late Mavis Palmer

• CONTENTS •

· ACKNOWLEDGMENTS ·

I am so grateful for the immense support network, both personal and professional, that allows me to write about money: My husband, Sujay Davé, who does so much, both visible and invisible, to support me and our family. My parents, Gail Shearer and Chris Palmer, who not only offer me endless encouragement, but also frequently take care of my children. My sisters and girlfriends for letting me bounce my ideas off them, even the terrible ones, and always responding with enthusiasm. My grandmothers, Janet Shearer Johnson and the late Mavis Palmer, to whom this book is dedicated, for showing me how to be a strong woman and mom. My former editors and colleagues at *U.S. News & World Report*; a working mom couldn't have a more supportive workplace and I am forever grateful, especially to Kim Castro.

My agent, Melissa Sarver White, is wonderful and I am so grateful we are now on our third book together. I thank the amazing editors and entire team at AMACOM, a fabulous publisher that I am so glad to be able to work with, especially my editor Stephen S. Power. I am also grateful for the support of the Journalists in Aging Fellowship, a collaboration of New America Media and the Gerontological Society of America, with support from AARP, which helped open my eyes to the specific challenges of older moms and how life choices early on can powerfully impact our later days.

ACKNOWLEDGMENTS

I thank all of the moms who generously shared their life experiences with me for this book, and who taught me so much along the way, as well as the financial professionals who shared their expertise and experiences with me. Over my nine years writing about money at *U.S. News & World Report,* I have interviewed hundreds of moms—many of them financial experts, too—about money. Some conversations are formal interviews; others more casual chats about work, budgets, and saving. All of them have informed this book, and I am grateful for their generosity.

As all moms know, there's always something that comes up to make the week a little more challenging. Pinkeye, flu, colds, ear infections, and snow days are just a few of the surprises that came our way as I wrote this book. At times, I fantasized about escaping to a writer's colony in the tropics, where I could write unimpeded for hours. But I did not really want that, of course, because escaping to such a place would require me to be away from the two little people I love more than anything; the ones who made me a mom and gave me so much inspiration to write this book. Kareena and Neal, I thank you for bringing joy into my life every day and for reminding me what really matters.

INTRODUCTION

INTO MOTHERHOOD

A s I sat facing the wood-paneled bar of one of Washington, D.C.'s most upscale restaurants, my two lunch companions, editors of a prestigious investing magazine, explained why they focus their financial coverage exclusively on older men. "They're our readers. Women aren't," they said. That's why, they continued, they don't cover topics that women investors might find of particular interest. The circular nature of this approach did not seem to bother them. Perhaps if they wrote about how to continue investing while you're taking a break from the workforce after the birth of a child, or how adding another child to your family might impact your financial goals, they might find that their publication would pull in a few more female readers.

As I carefully cut my roasted cauliflower while balancing a linen napkin on my lap, I wondered if our conversation represented a bigger problem in the financial industry. Historically, the industry has largely ignored women: Advertisements tend to feature older, graying men, with women serving as the arm candy. Fewer than one in four certified financial planners are women. In most investing and personal finance books, moms get nary a shout-out, and in the books that are written for us, which you can spot from their gleaming pink colors, the focus tends to be on how to shop less or coupon harder. It's insulting, really, when you start to think about it. Why do men get magazines and books on investing and getting rich while women get lectured on pinching pennies at the grocery store and cutting back on our shoe collections?

These messages fit us about as poorly as even the best pair of mom jeans. The reality is that we women—and moms especially —are handling a lot of money on a daily basis, and we're making financial decisions that affect not only us, but our families, too. Indeed, study after study finds that women and moms in partic- ular have oversize power when it comes to family money: Ac- cording to Fidelity, the vast majority (85 percent) of consumer purchases are made by women while we influence 95 percent of purchases of goods and services. By 2020, women will control two-thirds of the country's wealth, and 90 percent of us will be handling our finances on our own at some point in our lives, often as a result of death or divorce. We're bringing home more of the bacon, too: The Pew Research Center reports that in four out of ten households with children, moms are the only or pri- mary breadwinners. Similarly, the rise of blended families, single motherhood, and same-sex parents all contribute to the growing importance of women as the earners, savers, and investors within families.

At the same time, industry surveys show just how unhappy we are with the way the industry speaks to us. A report from the

Boston Consulting Group found that most women are dissatisfied with the level of service they are receiving from their financial services provider and many report feeling as if they are being talked down to by male advisers. I was not that surprised when a friend and (male) financial adviser recently told me, over coffee, that he overhead one of his young advisers talking directly to the husband while referring to the wife in third person—even though she was sitting right next to him. Given that kind of treatment, it's no surprise that 70 percent of women promptly replace their financial advisers within a year of becoming single. If you don't treat us like the financial powerhouses we are, we'll find someone else who does.

How exactly to do that, though, is complicated. I know from my own life and the experiences of my friends that moms face lots of unique financial concerns. Hardly a month goes by without at least one friend calling me to review salary negotiation tips in advance of an anticipated job offer, with rising child care costs always part of her budget calculations. My close girlfriends from college and I spent hours debating how much time to take off from work after each baby is born, in what capacity to return to work, and whether to continue to climb the career ladder as ambitiously once we are moms. (Each of us arrived at different— constantly changing—answers to that question.) Knowing I write about personal finance topics on a daily basis, my friends often email me all kinds of financial questions: How much life insurance do they need? Should they keep a separate bank account from their husband? How much money should they be saving?

When new babies arrive and families expand, the questions only grow more intense. As my younger sister, a family doctor in

San Francisco, prepared for the birth of her son, she had more questions about money than about birth. His arrival motivated her and her husband to review their retirement savings, decide whether to buy a house, and tackle other grown-up topics like writing a will. As she and so many other moms have experienced, the moment you become a parent your entire outlook, including on financial matters, changes. Suddenly, you're much more concerned with making sure your household is financially stable, that you can pay all of the monthly bills (including the new ones related to your baby), that you're saving for big future goals like college tuition, and that you'll be protected in the event of unexpected events, like a layoff or illness.

Even though I am immersed in these topics through my job, I frequently find myself stumped when it comes to certain financial questions myself, like how to afford child care once a second child arrives and how to financially prepare for an unpaid maternity leave. Once our son joined his big sister in our family, my credit card bills each month almost doubled. Between diapers, baby food, and random incidentals like baby sunscreen, I could hardly keep up with all of our new expenses. I also knew I needed to address bigger financial goals, like finding a way to grow my own income, as well as save for college and retirement amid the strain of those day-to-day expenses.

As any new mom can tell you, bringing home a tiny baby releases a rush of protective impulses: Did that sniffle indicate a major illness? Is the crib safe enough? Is the baby getting enough milk? Those impulses can and should extend to financial security, too. As moms, we have so much power to shape our families' wealth, both now and in the future, as our families grow up and get older. This book helps you make choices that lead to wealth, for yourself and your family. Together, we'll explore the specific questions and challenges that moms have and how to handle them, from working to saving and investing to teaching your children financial smarts from the beginning. We'll get to know the strategies and secrets of dozens of smart moms, who are making savvy choices for themselves and their families. The chapters and handbook in the back of the book include checklists, templates, and action steps.

The truth is, many of us set ourselves up for a path to richness—or poorness—long before we become moms, before we're even aware of the financial power we wield, and those trajectories can be hard, but not impossible, to change. The spending and saving habits we develop in our twenties, the life partner we select (if any), the career we pursue—all these decisions have a momentous impact on our future wealth levels. That's why I sometimes spend my lunch break texting with my youngest sister, urging her to skip the $50 massage and instead learn to relax in less expensive ways after a bad day, in between offering her dating advice and career guidance. (I'm a full-service sister.)

It's also why I find it so disturbing every time a new survey comes out showing that young women tend to lag behind young men when it comes to basic financial literacy. At one event held on Capitol Hill, researchers from Wells Fargo explained that women in their twenties already feel less satisfied and less optimistic about finances than their male peers. They are also more likely to say they feel "overwhelmed" by their debt—and, in fact, for good reason: They have more of it than young men. Twenty-something women earn less, save less, and invest less than their male counterparts: Millennial men report more investable assets than millennial women by almost double the amount ($58,500 compared to $31,400).

An international survey of over 29,000 fifteen-year-olds in eighteen countries conducted by the Organization for Economic Cooperation and Development (OECD) found that even at that young age, girls demonstrate lower levels of financial literacy and confidence in their abilities than boys. Girls earned lower scores on math questions and reported higher levels of anxiety toward math. Differences start to appear before puberty: A 2014 T. Rowe Price survey of children between the ages of eight and fourteen found that boys are more likely than girls to talk to their parents about financial goals and more likely to consider themselves "smart about money."

It's no wonder, then, that twenty years later, when we're moms ourselves, we report lower levels of confidence when it comes to money. A 2015 Fidelity survey of 1,542 adult women found that most say they are uncomfortable talking about finances, even with friends, spouses, or financial professionals. The majority of the women surveyed said they want to be more involved when it comes to managing their money, but just 28 percent said they felt confident picking investments and 37 percent felt confident handling retirement planning.

In fact, it's motherhood itself that is likely to create some of the biggest financial stresses we'll face in our lives. Not only are children expensive, but they can turn our lives upside down—making it harder to keep a job or keep up with bills. Before she entered politics and was elected a U.S. senator, Elizabeth Warren's research on bankruptcy showed that being a mom is the single best predictor of financial ruin, with the highest risk for single moms.

Given those dismal facts, it's time for us moms to have as much targeted guidance on building wealth as we receive on dropping that so-called baby weight, reducing wrinkles, or saving $10 on our next bulk order of laundry detergent. Contrary to my dining companions' perspective at that eye-opening lunch, our experience with life and money is different from that of our fathers, brothers, sons, and husbands, and it's just as important. From the perspective of our children, it's possibly even more important, since we're the ones calling the money shots most of the time. So much of our children's well-being, financial and otherwise, depends on us. The decisions that we make today affect whether they can count on the stability of a family home and meal every day, sign up for their favorite (and pricey) after-school activities, and attend college without taking on a crippling amount of student loan debt.

With the right guidance, we can harness our financial power to create a richer life for ourselves and our families. A richer life that includes not only more money in the bank, but the freedom to make choices that reflect our biggest goals and dreams for ourselves, our families, and our communities.

After that meeting, I decided to dive further into the trenches, to talk to moms in the real world who are making those financial decisions for themselves and their families every day. Regardless of what the financial industry thinks, moms are the real power players when it comes to managing the money of American families. Specifically, I wanted to uncover the secrets of smart moms who make financial decisions that lead to security and wealth for their families. I knew that I, and other moms, could learn a lot from them—and I did, even more than I could have predicted. In fact, in the course of my research I ended up making some significant changes to my own financial life—from little things, like always bringing my wallet on family outings, even if I knew my husband had his, to bigger ones, like being more involved in managing my family's long-term savings and investments, especially those dedicated to future college tuition payments. (In fact, after doing the research for Chapter 5, I actually opened a 529 account for each of my children for the first time.) Instead of happily letting my husband maintain our password-protected master spreadsheet of our various accounts and loans, I downloaded it to my own computer (and made sure I knew the password). I also started talking about money much more with my daughter (and will do the same with my son when he is a bit older), because I learned how much of an impact those conversations can have. I asked my own parents about their finances, too, so I am more prepared to help them in the future, as they get older.

Smart moms, I learned, might look just like any other mother you run into in the carpool line. But if you looked at their bank accounts, credit card statements, and in their wallets, you would see some distinctive traits: Smart moms always earn their own money, even if it drops significantly during their child-rearing years. Smart moms have enough short-term cash in the bank so that they can handle unexpected expenses or temporary drops in income; they prioritize short-term savings and have paid off all high-interest-rate debt. They have insurance policies in place that would cover them in the event of a tragedy. Smart moms model wealth-producing behavior for their own sons and daughters, who develop smart financial habits early. Smart moms don't hesitate to make purchases that they know will benefit their own well-being or that of their families. They are actively involved in their own savings and investment decisions and do not hand over the money management reins to partners. Smart moms have clear money and life goals that they are constantly progressing toward, even at a slow pace. They feel comfortable and confident talking about their finances; managing money is as familiar and even as enjoyable to them as slipping into a warm bath.

No matter how much or how little they have, their money gives them and their families a sense of security. Being a smart mom is not about earning above a certain amount of money, amassing a specific net worth, or owning a million-dollar home. The smart moms featured here include teachers, nurses, and freelance writers, along with lawyers, business owners, and financial professionals. They span single moms, young moms, and older moms. Regardless of their income or savings level, what they have in common is the comfort, confidence, and safety that comes from making smart money choices.

The following chapters reveal secret strategies, tips, and advice from smart moms, giving you the game plan that will help you build the wealth and life that you and your family deserve.

1

SAVE (AND SPEND) LIKE A MOTHER

I have a friend on Facebook who routinely posts photos of her hauls at the grocery store, along with how shockingly little all those bags of chips and paper towels cost. While impressive—she usually brings home a full trunk load of items for less than $50—I can't help but wonder if her effort is worth those savings. She spends hours clipping paper coupons (a habit she also shares with her Facebook friends) and then ends up with enough frozen pork chops to survive the apocalypse (as long as her freezer keeps running). Would her time be better spent on a more strategic financial task, like filing flex-spending receipts for health care costs or rebalancing her retirement investments? Will her family even eat all those pork chops before they go bad? Will they want to?

Our culture celebrates penny-pinching moms on television shows like TLC's *Extreme Couponing*. The Great Recession made frugality cool again, and that's a good thing—there's no reason to spend more than we need to on running our households. As the editor of the popular *U.S. News* blog "The Frugal Shopper," I enjoyed spreading the word about how to snag the best deals and cut expenses. I take great pleasure myself in typing in a coupon code when shopping online that automatically takes $20 or more off my bill.

But there's a dark side of penny-pinching, too, especially when it falls to moms to track coupons and hunt down discounts. It keeps us focused on small, short-term savings instead of working on the far more significant financial strategies that can really build our family's wealth over time. We get a rush from saving $5 at checkout while leaving $500 on the table because we didn't sign up for a flex-spending account at work to pay for child care expenses or we left our long-term savings in an account with zero return.

I was struck by this paradox while watching an episode of *The Real Housewives of Beverly Hills,* where one of the stars, Brandi Glanville, tells the camera that she wants to make a lot of money to create stability for her children and ensure she never depends on a man for money again. (Her ex-husband, the actor Eddie Cibrian, cheated on her and then married LeAnn Rimes, a frequent plot point on the show.) I wanted to give her a high-five for her financial ambition.

But then, later in the episode, when she cashes in a six-figure check from her bestselling book, she uses it to splurge on a six-figure custom car, instead of investing her windfall for her (and her children's) future. This is the same woman who tweets about her own successful couponing binges; according to her Twitter feed, she saved more than $70 with coupons on one trip to the grocery store. Impressive, like my Facebook friends, but she would do better to buy a much cheaper car and not worry so much about the dollars and cents saved on food.

That's why we have to break out of this restrictive couponing mind-set and think bigger—much bigger. Think about how to be a skilled shopper every day and not just a discount chaser on the weekends. Think about negotiating ongoing bills and monthly expenses, instead of getting distracted by onetime purchases that aren't that expensive anyway. We should think about investing the savings that we do generate in a way that grows that money instead of spending it on some other forgettable purchase that will soon turn into house clutter.

Moms, it turns out, have a hugely important role to play when it comes to family spending, mostly because we're doing so much of it. We make the vast majority of consumer purchases ourselves, and those choices are much bigger than just which laundry detergent to put in the cart. A 2014 Wells Fargo survey found that among women with at least $250,000 in assets, 82 percent are in charge of their family's day-to-day finances, including budgeting and spending decisions. That's a lot of pressure on our shoulders. Luckily, we can handle it, and certain strategies can help ease the burden of constantly searching out the best deal while also handling the more long-term aspects of our family finances, too.

Approaching our spending with an attitude of frugal luxury, whether it's a weeknight dinner or annual vacation, means finding the best that we can afford for our family while getting the lowest price for it. In the movie *The Hundred-Foot Journey,* starring Helen Mirren as a grumpy French restaurant owner in hot pursuit of a second Michelin star, Mirren's character accuses an older gentleman of being cheap, and therefore poor, because he negotiated the rate on his hotel room. He replies that asking for a discount just means that he is thrifty, not poor. That's a truth moms know, too. And they feel comfortable asking for those discounts when it matters, because they know they (and their families) deserve them, along with the wealth that those discounts generate over time.

SMARTER SHOPPING

Every year around the winter holidays, I call Kit Yarrow, a consumer psychologist and an expert on shopping, to get her advice on how to handle the annual shopping frenzy and still come out ahead. As a smart shopper herself, she always teaches me something new about getting the most out of retailers, and as a mother herself (her two children are now grown), she developed her own routines and strategies that work for family life.

One of the first things she taught me is that you have to step away from all the enticements that retailers send in your direction. It sounds counterintuitive, since it feels like walking into that half-off sale will reap big discounts, or that getting daily emails about sales will direct you toward savings, but all that noise actually makes you spend more, because you feel pressure to buy things that you really don't need. Anytime you see a "half-off" sign or a "one-day only" sale, Yarrow suggests walking away, unless the item was already on your shopping list.

Those kind of sales, Yarrow says, "churn up emotions like competitiveness, the fear of missing out, or a sense of urgency. Those emotions cloud thinking and you want to be sharp when you're spending money." Since so much of this temptation comes in the form of emails today, consider unsubscribing from all those retailer emails guaranteed to make sure you never miss a sale. Missing sales can actually be a good thing for your bank account.

That's also why scrolling through shopping apps on your smartphone is not the best relaxation activity after you get the kids to bed. "People use trolling for bargains as a hobby. It's what knitting would have been forty years ago—a mindless activity to allow your mind to relax," Yarrow says, noting that people often shop on their phones or online during lunch hours at work or in the evenings. As she knows from her own behavior as well as her research, "the more bargain-focused you are, the more money you spend." Bargains, she says, give us a false sense of control over our chaotic lives.

To regain control without spending, the first line of defense is to maintain an ongoing shopping list of all the items you actually need to buy. That way, if you know you need a new coffeemaker, you can be on the lookout for deals on the kind of coffeemaker you want and anticipate the upcoming expense. You can take your time, comparing the pros and cons of different models, and end up with the best quality product for your money. (If you have a partner, you both can be involved in the process, and then neither person will be surprised by the bill when it comes.)

Another smart strategy is to go to the discounts, instead of letting them come to you. Rather than being the passive recipient of retailers' emails and smartphone push notifications that let you know about daily deals, you can seek out the best price when you are ready to purchase one of the items off your list. Popular coupon tools and price comparison apps like RetailMeNot, PriceGrabber, RedLaser, and Brad's Deals make it easy to search for discount codes and other deals once you are ready to buy, as opposed to directing you to buy when you might not be ready. For online shopping, browser add-ons like PriceBlink or InvisibleHand let you know if another site has a lower price for an item you are about to buy. The difference is that you are the one in control of the timing and not adapting your schedule to the retailers' calendars. That's why I also like to use Unroll.Me, an email unsubscribe tool that automatically pulls all mass emails, including ads from retailers, into a single "rollup" email each day, to prevent you from getting constantly pinged all day long. (When I first signed up, I was shocked to see that I had unknowingly subscribed to over 150 mass email lists!)

Deciding what belongs on that list can be tricky. Do you really need a new handbag, or is your current one, despite its worn appearance, still doing the job? Do your children need new clothes or would hand-me-downs work as well? What messages do our choices tell our children about value and worth? In one of my favorite country songs, "American Middle Class," Angaleena Presley sings about remembering her mom gluing Keds logos on the back of her white shoes so they looked like real Keds. Now, decades later and a mom herself, she feels almost nostalgic about those days and proud of her mom's creativity, which didn't stop with shoes. "She would cut the Guess patch off a pair of jeans and sew it onto a pair that she got from a yard sale," she recalls.

While the singer is no longer pressed for cash—in addition to her solo career, she is part of the successful trio Pistol Annies with superstar Miranda Lambert—she still copies her mom's strategy in her own home. "What my mom taught me, and what I still do, is, if you don't have it, you can make it," Angaleena says. In fact, she told her husband that for Christmas one year, instead of gifts, she wanted to fix up the old items around their house.

UP FOR GRABS

An equally important shopping technique comes into play after you have purchased a product or service that doesn't live up to your standards in some way. It's one that a lot of moms struggle with, because it can require awkward and potentially time-consuming conversations. But it saves me a couple thousand dollars each year, mostly related to health insurance, flex spending, and retail purchases, like defective clothing. The fact is big companies, from insurers to clothing stores, make mistakes, and most of them probably go uncontested. It's only the customers who speak up who get their money back.

One of my favorite ongoing expenses is Stitch Fix, an online personal shopping service that sends you a custom box of clothes each month, tailored to your own preferences and size. Since I don't have time to shop on the weekends and the service offers high quality at a reasonable price, it's what keeps me feeling presentable at the office. One month, though, two buttons fell off the tops that I bought through the service. At first, I just let it go and planned to try to sew the buttons on myself later. But the more I thought about it, the more I realized that I should let the company know. After all, I'm a loyal customer, and they should know the buttons are falling off their tops after minimal wear. So I sent a note and got a $16 refund. Quick emails to retailers like this almost always result in some kind of refund or future discount. I sent a similar email to Tide detergent after the company unexpectedly changed the scent on me. Tide quickly sent me a $20 coupon for a new jug of detergent. These amounts are too small to spend too much time on them, but worth a quick email or two.

Similarly, I never complete an online purchase without first doing a quick web search for the retailer's name and the words "coupon" or "promo code." At least half the time, this search leads me to a code that gets me $5 off or more. That's money I would have otherwise paid without even realizing I could have kept it, and it takes less than a minute.

My most significant savings usually come from health insurance claims that are improperly processed. Recently, my insurer rejected the expenses of a routine physical because it falsely thought I had already had a physical that year. It took multiple phone calls, but I eventually got the charges dropped. Following up with customer service is a pain, but the savings can be worth the effort. Reviewing your credit card statement, as well as any statements from insurers, for potential errors can help alert you to problems. When you call or email to follow up, be sure to take notes; be persistent; and, if necessary, complain about the problem publicly on social media, like Twitter or Facebook, taking care to "tag" the company to maximize the public impact. I don't like publicly shaming companies in front of their customers, but if they're not fixing an error, following up in a public forum can be the only way to get them motivated to help you out. (Just be mindful to avoid libelous statements that could leave you vulnerable to a lawsuit.) This social media approach has helped me get refunds on my Comcast cable bill and a quicker update from my electric company on when my power was coming back on after a storm. For extra help alerting you to potential fraud or errors on your credit card, you can also download BillGuard, an app that relies on crowdsourcing among its one million–plus members to flag potential problems and resolve disputes between customers and companies.

As a last resort, if the company is failing to resolve the dispute with you, even after public shaming on social media, then I recommend filing an official complaint with the federal government (the Consumer Financial Protection Bureau has an online complaint tracking system for troubles related to the financial services industry) or through the Better Business Bureau, an industry group. After exhausting all other available resources when trying to get a new and corrected birth certificate for my newborn son (issued through the private company that contracts with the District of Columbia government), I filed a complaint with the Better Business Bureau. The problem, which had gone on for months and taken multiple phone calls and letters in my sleep-deprived state, was resolved almost immediately. (By the way, the same strategy applies to getting paid, if you take on any kind of freelance or contract work that doesn't come with a steady direct deposit. You often have to track down payments with the same focused determination that you have to put toward getting your money from retailers. The payoff is worth it, though, because it literally puts money in your bank account.)

For the most part, this strategy comes down to speaking up at the right moment and not wasting any time or energy feeling self-conscious about it. I once watched a thirtysomething guy in a business suit negotiate the price of his cappuccino with the barista at my favorite coffee shop. He had brought in his own mug, which he thought entitled him to a discount. He didn't get the discount, but no one minded that he asked. We ladies need more of that sense of entitlement in our own lives, the kind that leads us to ask for a better deal on everything, from coffee to cars. Otherwise, we're leaving money that belongs to our families on the table.

SPENDING BOOTCAMP

Several years ago, I met a young woman—let's call her Emily—who was a recovering shopaholic. She confided this information casually, while we were at a work-sponsored baseball game, as if she were sharing that she preferred hot chocolate to lattes. As we talked more, though, it soon became clear that this experience still weighed heavily on her daily life and had even threatened to undo her closest relationships.

Her shopping addiction, she explained, stemmed from a lack of self-worth and really took root during a bad relationship. Buying a new outfit gave her a temporary confidence boost and made her feel more beautiful, she explained. But even after leaving that relationship and marrying a supportive husband, her shopping addiction stuck with her. She found herself sneaking shopping bags into her closet, so her husband wouldn't see all that she had spent, and racking up massive credit card bills that she couldn't afford. Eventually, with her husband's help after she came clean to him, she stopped relying on shopping as a way to feel good and adopted a healthier relationship with money.

Letting go of bad habits, even when you know you need to, can be painfully difficult, especially because those habits have often grown out of deep feelings and beliefs about ourselves. That point was really driven home to me by Kerry Cohen, the editor of *Spent: Exposing Our Complicated Relationship with Shopping*, a collection of essays by women about shopping. "We often spend because we're trying to fulfill a deep need, even a hurt that goes back to our earliest memories," she says. In the essays, women recount over and over again buying things—and overspending—because they are trying to feel the same kind of love they used to feel as children, when parents were taking care of them, buying them what they needed.

Kerry shares in the book that when her parents got divorced when she was a young girl and her mom moved to a different country, shopping became a way for her to feel loved. She recalls that her dad would go shopping with her in department stores out of guilt. Then, as an adult and mom herself, she found herself once again turning to shopping when going through her own divorce.

Taking control of spending, then, often means addressing some deeper need and taking care of ourselves emotionally and building a sense of security and self-worth. "When I feel that desire to shop and know I can't or shouldn't, I look at what's happening with me emotionally or otherwise and try to care for that part instead. Sometimes it simply means looking at everything I already have and feeling the blessing of that," she says. (Kerry also says she constantly talks to her own children about resisting the marketing messages of commercials to help break the cycle.) That cultivation of a feeling of gratitude for all you have is a sentiment I heard expressed over and over again from the moms I interviewed.

Changing habits takes time, though, and taking small steps, like cutting your shopping budget in half each month until you get to a number that fits your budget, is easier than suddenly allowing yourself no more new shoes. Charles Duhigg, author of *The Power of Habit,* says you have to reward yourself when you are replacing a bad habit. Instead of just taking a prior source of pleasure away from yourself, give yourself something just as fun to increase the likelihood of the habit sticking. So instead of mindlessly shopping deals on your iPhone at night, find a new TV series to enjoy, browse a magazine, or read a good book.

Moms can't stop shopping altogether, though—we're constantly picking up items for our kids and our homes. Some mornings I feel like I barely get out of bed before I need to buy my son a new sunscreen stick for school or my daughter more headbands. Being selective without being stingy is our daily challenge. Sometimes I think a different part of my brain is making purchases for my children versus for myself; I can easily spend $50 on new tops for my daughter with a few clicks on my computer while agonizing over a new work shirt for the same price for myself. (For more help navigating the "must have" versus "waste of money" purchase, check out "Purse Check: What to Ask Before You Buy," a series of questions in the handbook section at the back of the book.)

If you are carrying any credit card debt from month to month, then it's especially important to commit to a spending shift, for yourself and your family. Focusing on everything you want to say "yes" to instead of what you're constantly denying yourself can help, too. Every time you say "no" to a new pair of shoes, you're saying yes to a bigger savings account, a future activity with your child, or perhaps a new home one day. Whatever is on your "yes" list—your dreams, financial and otherwise, which we will discuss in more detail in the next chapter—is what you're getting closer to when you opt against more short-term splurges. If you are a visual person, you might even want to make a collage of those goals and keep it nearby to remind yourself of them when you feel tempted.

SMART MOM, RICH MOM
CREDIT CARD RULES

CREDIT CARDS ARE LIKE high school boyfriends: some are reliable and supportive but most are not worth your time (or your money). While there's no single card that's best for all moms, a few guiding principles will help make sure you are maximizing your rewards while minimizing your costs. Comparison sites like NerdWallet.com or CreditCards.com can also help you find a card that will keep you happy. (*U.S. News* has a credit card comparison site at money.usnews.com/credit-cards.)

Avoid annual fees. Cards with annual fees, even for airline perks that you know you'll use, are rarely worth the price. That's because you can almost always buy these perks yourself for less than the cost of the annual fees involved.

Check the interest rate. If you carry any debt at all, then it makes the most sense to use a credit card that offers the lowest rate available so that you're minimizing your monthly payments while you make a plan to pay off that debt.

Get rewards. If you pay off your bill in full each month, then you can take advantage of credit card perks, including identity theft protection and rewards points, without paying the price. Make sure you are using a card that gives you rewards you will use, including cash back or gift cards to your favorite stores. If you have reward options, the most efficient choice is usually cash, directly deposited into your bank account or redeemed as a credit on your card.

Protect yourself. Many cards come with added protections, like travel insurance, and if you're a frequent traveler, then using these cards could save you money.

Improve your score. Credit scores, which determine the loan rate you get on anything from a mortgage to a car loan, are influenced by your credit card history as well as other types of bills. Make sure you are keeping your score as high as possible by making on-time payments each month on all your accounts. At least once a year, get your credit report through AnnualCreditReport.com to check for any errors that have popped up. Review your credit card statement each month to make sure all charges are valid. The first sign of identity theft is often an erroneous charge.

Pay off your debt. Smart moms don't carry credit card debt, because it's expensive and its existence suggests something is out of whack with your spending. They have emergency savings funds to cover unexpected costs like a hospital bill or car repair, and they don't waste their money paying credit card interest rates and fees. If you are carrying around debt, then make a plan to pay it off within the next year, by cutting costs and directing the money toward the debt, starting with the highest interest rate accounts.

You don't have to adopt a Spartan-like attitude toward your material possessions or even deny yourself the pleasures of this consumer-driven economy. Some of my best purchases in the last year have been material ones: a new handbag that helps me stay organized, comfortable and stylish boots, new workout clothes. Sometimes, we moms are so busy buying things for our kids that we forget to spend on ourselves, even on the things that can improve our overall family life. On one trip to the grocery store to pick up an item I had forgotten to order, I remember watching all the moms in the dreary parking lot, loading bags into the trunks of their cars, and I couldn't help but wonder what else we could be doing with our time. For about $10, we can get our groceries delivered and spend the time playing with our kids, exercising, or finishing a household project instead. Anything that helps ease our own stresses and well-being is an investment in our families, too.

These tips emerged from my conversations with moms about their shopping habits:

- Focus on buying items that improve your life in some way. You can also reduce clutter around your home—and keep your monthly credit card bill down—by avoiding purchases you (and your families) won't really use.

- Invest in services that save time and energy and improve family life, such as grocery delivery or Amazon Prime.

- Stick up for yourself, and your family, by speaking up when you've been unfairly charged or receive a damaged product or unsatisfactory service.

- Gravitate toward self-care activities that don't come with a massive cost, including exercise, reading, cooking, and making art. Gear spending toward experiences rather than things.

- Occasionally splurge on items that make you feel good. Smart moms make room in their budget for the occasional pick-me-up, whether it's the latest Taylor Swift album or a new moisturizer. I know one mom who says her sanity depends on her monthly hair removal appointment at a local spa on Sunday mornings. To each her own. My own favorite busy mama indulgences involve using lunchtime for a quick pedicure and purchasing monthly beauty treats from Birchbox for $10.

◆ Get the lowest price available on items through savvy shopping, including the latest price comparison apps and websites that alert you to lower prices. Before making any online purchase, check around the website for advertisements related to discounts or free shipping codes. If nothing comes up, do a web search with the name of the retailer and the word "coupon"; it often will lead you to a discount code. I saved 10 percent off new bedding for my son just by signing up for the company's newsletter (and then I promptly added the emails to my daily "rollup" through Unroll.Me).

◆ Don't waste money on credit card fees or interest rates; instead, pay off bills in full each month and on time through automated payments.

MAMA BEAR SAVINGS

Now that we've streamlined our shopping habits, it's time to leverage that money by managing our savings. Short-term savings, or any money we want for emergencies and monthly expenses, should be in an easily accessible, low-risk liquid account. By definition, that means it will come with a low interest rate, but that doesn't mean you need to give up on getting any perks from your savings account. Your primary bank account should offer FDIC protection (meaning up to $250,000 is insured), no monthly or annual fees, an online interface for easy transfers, a secure app for your mobile devices, and automated services like transfers into higher interest rate accounts and bill pay. A service like MaxMyInterest.com automatically shifts your money into the highest interest rate account available, while maintaining FDIC protection. A secondary account for emergency savings and expenses over the next few years also belongs in a low-risk, no fee, liquid account that earns a return, even if it's low. Money market funds can work well. (Longer-term savings and investments belong in more aggressive securities, which we'll discuss in Chapter 2.)

If you have access to a credit union, and most Americans do (aSmarterChoice.org can show you which ones), then that's another good option for your short-term savings. Credit unions tend to offer slightly higher interest rates on savings (as well as lower rates on loans) and similar protections.

If credit cards are like boyfriends, then banks are like husbands. They're usually with you for the long haul, so you want to choose carefully and consider many factors, not just the superficial ones. If your current bank isn't meeting your needs, because it's charging fees or you don't like the online interface, then shop around for a better one. You deserve it. Comparison websites like Google Compare, Bankrate.com, and FindABetterBank.com can all help connect you with Mr. Right (Bank).

Saving well is a skill, like the ability to find a flattering bathing suit style or developing the patience to withstand a two-year-old's tantrum. Once you have a well of savings, then you can focus on achieving your biggest personal and family goals—the topic of our next chapter.

SMART MOM, RICH MOM
ACTION STEPS

1. Take some time to reflect on your purchases this week. Did you splurge on items that made you feel good or improve your life in some way? If you notice yourself using shopping as your "go to" pick-me-up, then find a less expensive serotonin-booster, like a cup of coffee or a hot bubble bath. Spending on experiences rather than material goods tends to produce the biggest boost to our overall happiness levels—and creates lasting family memories. One of the best ways to get insight into how you're currently spending is to track every expenditure for a month. Write down everything you buy, from food to shampoo to coffee. (You can do this manually on paper or use a free tool like Mint.com to do it for you.) You might be surprised to discover that hundreds of dollars each month are going toward takeout that you didn't even really enjoy or toys that your kids play with once and then forget about.

2. Use online comparison-shopping tools that help save you money on big purchases and get bulk discounts on regular household purchases like soap, paper towels, and even pantry items. Using Amazon Subscribe and Save and other similar services can reduce monthly costs.

3. Reduce clutter and temptation in your email inbox with a service like Unroll.Me or by unsubscribing to retailers' promotional emails.

4. Next time a retailer, insurance company, or small business overcharges you or provides a product or service that is subpar in some way, send an email explaining the situation and asking for a refund. Follow up by phone or social media.

5. If you have credit card debt or a tendency to overshop, then give yourself an intervention. Before buying anything, ask yourself if you'll still appreciate it in six months, and wait at least twenty-four hours before buying any nonessential items. Keep tabs on your credit report, too, by reviewing your free credit report annually (at annualcreditreport.com) and correcting any errors.

6. Manage your savings like they're the crown jewels, because to you and your family, they are. Make sure they are in a safe and secure place that is easily accessible and earning at least a modest return. Automate monthly savings transfers from your paycheck and once a year review their growth and consider whether it's time to transfer a portion into a more aggressive, long-term investment account.

2

OWNING IT

The path to becoming a smart mom starts long before the birth of your first child, and even before the double lines of a pregnancy test appear. Just as prenatal vitamins help us build our reserves of iron and folic acid, certain money habits adopted early make us stronger and better prepared for the financial shock of family life. Many of the moms I interviewed had been saving money since their first job, practicing frugal habits until they became second nature, and even making investments while still in their twenties with their futures in mind.

When I asked two moms—both lawyers in their mid-thirties who earn the biggest paychecks in their marriages and who have seven kids between them—just how they got so comfortable with money, they talked about the first jobs that they held as teenagers. One of them had just explained to me how she negotiated a signing bonus worth twice as much as a luxury car. She said that as the daughter of parents of modest means living in the affluent suburbs of Washington, D.C., she started working at a dry cleaners to earn spending money. That, she says, helped teach her the value of hard work—and instilled in her the deep desire to eventually find her way to more powerful and lucrative jobs. She buckled down and went to college, then law school, and landed jobs at prestigious law firms and impressive clerkships. Today, married to a teacher, she handles her family's money, including investments. "My husband doesn't even know how to log into our checking account," she jokes. (Of course, he should probably make sure he learns those passwords, so he can handle their affairs on his own if he has to, just as any mom should.)

The other lawyer, Lindsay Kelly, shared a similar story. Growing up with parents who never completed high school, she committed herself to success early and started by working at a Subway as a teenager. She balanced her mom's checkbook for her and convinced her parents to take her to Disney World in tenth grade by creating a budget on her own and showing it to them. She also handles the money and investments in her own household—her husband, she says, doesn't keep track of what bills are due and when, and which account to use to pay them.

Neither woman could remember their parents explicitly discussing money with them, but both watched their parents work hard and live within their means. They both wanted more for themselves and their own families—success, money, prestige— and they embraced that ambition fully, and today both women are reaping the financial benefits. They ask for more money when they take new jobs, invest aggressively for their future goals, and save more than they spend—habits they've been practicing since they were teenagers. They don't waste time worrying whether they are "worth" their high incomes or whether they deserve the financial security that they've built, and they don't hand over money management to their husbands. They just do it themselves, without reservations.

For many moms, though, our relationship with money is as complicated and fraught as how we feel about our bodies. We have dark issues we have to work through, some of which date back to childhood and how we watched our own moms manage, or not manage, their finances.

My interviews with even the most successful moms—women I see as role models—showed me over and over again how women sometimes have to go through extreme financial hardship before finding their way. Gail Sheehy, author of the bestselling book *Passages*, recalls living off of spaghetti for weeks on end when she was a working journalist and single mom in her twenties and early thirties, as she started to write what would become her bestselling (and high-earning) book. "Being a single mom in the 1960s was not cool, and I was too proud to ask for alimony," she says. "I really had to assume the breadwinner role for my daughter and myself," she says. She paid $139 in rent a month and hired a housekeeper who also served as a surrogate mother to her young daughter as she traveled for her reporting. She estimates that she lived on about $15,000 for two years. "I ran out of money," she recalls.

That all changed with the publication of *Passages*, which sold millions of copies around the world. She bought what was then an inexpensive old farmhouse in East Hampton for herself and her daughter, where they would take refuge for the next thirty years, before she sold it for a hefty profit. While she's faced other financial challenges, most notably when she scaled back her work to care for her ailing husband, Clay Felker, Sheehy, now in her mid-seventies, enjoys relative financial security from her book earnings as well as the fact that she continues to work, well past what most people consider to be retirement age.

Most moms, though, don't enjoy million-dollar windfalls. In fact, one of the richest mothers I know—in the fullest sense of that word—is a mom who is proud of her relatively modest income as a teacher and writer. I first encountered Alison Singh Gee in the pages of *Entertainment Weekly*, which featured her memoir, "Where the Peacocks Sing," with a teaser that referred to a young journalist in Hong Kong who meets her "Prince Charming" and follows him to India. I downloaded her book onto my Kindle that night.

As I read her tale of meeting her husband and traveling to his family's dilapidated palace in an Indian village, I was struck by how much of her story was really about consciously changing some very bad money habits. Habits so ingrained that they seemed to drive her into the arms of men who were not right for her, and to hold on to a life characterized by materialism instead of something deeper and more meaningful. She spent much of her twenties living the high life as an ex-pat in Hong Kong, dating men who showered her with gifts and funded her luxe lifestyle. What is riveting about her story, though, is that when she meets her future husband, Ajay, she consciously rejects her life of fancy restaurants and expensive art. She realizes Ajay has something else, something much better to offer—his love, and incidentally, his status as Indian royalty.

The process of adapting to her new and more affordable lifestyle didn't happen quickly, and she acknowledges the struggle. "I had to confront that it wasn't going to be easy anymore. It was tremendously painful," she told me when I caught up with her by phone. She had to get used to taking public buses instead of taxis and to cooking more instead of eating out all the time. She started going on more walks to replace the time she used to spend shopping.

Alison says her lust for material items dates back to her childhood, where, she says, "it felt like there was never enough"— enough love or enough pizza slices. Sometimes, there wasn't enough money for new shoes, even when they were needed, but sometimes her dad would splurge on lobster. "We inherit so much from our parents. Not just genetics and our houses, but a financial point of view," she says. Her parents always told her to marry rich and didn't teach her how to budget or live within her means herself.

She eventually learned to cultivate a deep sense of security and satisfaction from the life she built in Los Angeles with her husband, which includes being a mom to their daughter and a new career as an instructor of creative writing at the UCLA Extension program. She consciously seeks the feeling of abundance by appreciating what she has. "Maybe what we're really after is a richness of experience and family life. How rich are we to have the creative, loving, adventurous life we have?" she says. Sometimes, after dinner, she talks with her preteen daughter about being grateful for what they have: "We have a nice meal, but we make it at home. We get to put our own ingredients into the food and take herbs from our garden, and we can sit at our dining room table for hours. Same with watching movies—we could spend $35 to $40 going to the movies, or we could get a DVD and make popcorn and everyone gets to watch together." All of that, and talking with her daughter about it, helps create a feeling of richness—not of material goods, but of family life, she says.

Now, Alison says, "I believe in fewer things but better things. I know experience and health are the most valuable." She and her husband own their house, which she says adds to "our sense of luxury in everyday life," and they're currently squirreling away savings for a major renovation. She still buys Anthropologie dresses, but only on sale. "That's how I go about affording luxury—by being a savvy shopper."

ALL IN

No matter where you start, or whether you're already a mom to teenagers or on the verge of giving birth, getting on the smart mom path begins with getting clear on your goals.

Those goals set the stage for everything else that we talk about. Your goals are like your favorite pair of leggings—some are colorful, others pretty basic, and they're always stretching and changing to fit your life. They should feel comfortable, but also prod you toward your best self by making it easier for you to exercise or not get stressed when your son wipes his muddy hands on them. But sometimes you need new ones. At the very least, you should regularly review whether it's time for an upgrade. Even the best made goals, and leggings, probably don't last much beyond five years.

I tend to review my goals at least once a year, usually in the fall, as the new calendar year approaches. I take a vacation day, organize my children's winter clothes, and think about where I want to be in one, five, and ten years. What would make me feel like I'm living a "rich" life—not just financially, although that's a part of it. Would I feel "rich" by having $10,000 more in the bank, by taking a family trip to the beach, or by changing careers? The five- and ten-year goals are usually pretty fuzzy, but slowly come into focus over time: I want to earn more money and have more cash in the bank. I want to take my family to Japan and Ireland. The next year's goals are much more honed: Write this book. Speak about money at two or more events. Cook healthier meals for my kids, featuring two veggies at each dinner. Run and practice yoga four times a week. Sleep seven to eight hours a night. Go on two dates a month with my husband. Put at least 15 percent of my income into my retirement account and start a college savings fund for our two children.

Your own goals probably won't all revolve explicitly around money, but almost all of our goals relate to finances in some way. Money is the undercurrent of our lives; it's what lets us do stuff or limits our choices. And certain goals, like a career change, affect our income. Write your answers to the following questions in a notebook that you keep handy to remind yourself of your goals.

What would make you feel like a rich mom? How do you define wealth—financially and otherwise? Examples include reaching a certain savings level, travel, and lifestyle choices like affording private school for your kids, going on vacation once a year, or making a significant donation to a worthy cause.

What do you want to accomplish, financially and otherwise, in the next year? Examples include saving $10,000, putting $15,000 into a retirement account, starting a college savings account, or getting a new job.

What about in the next five years? Ten years? Examples include taking a big family trip, earning a new professional certification, or buying a new house.

Once you get specific about your goals, it's easier to see what aspect of money management to tackle first. If your big long-term dream is to take a family trip overseas in five years, then you'll want to start slipping money into a savings account or conservative investment account. If your top priority is paying off credit card debt, then you'll send in monthly payments before putting money toward longer-term savings goals. If you're planning a career change that will lead to a decrease in income, then you'll want to revamp your budget now to reflect that decrease in cash flow. Or you might look at your list and decide those goals will not be realized on your current income alone, so it's time to launch a side business or otherwise grow your income (or cut your spending). Recognizing and expressing what you need is the first step to getting it.

Saving is usually a big component, too. Saving is a habit, like eating broccoli on a regular basis. If you weren't brought up thinking of roasted veggies as a tasty side dish, then it will be harder for you to get into the idea as an adult—just ask George

H. W. Bush. You can still do it, and even develop your own custom recipe (red pepper flakes, anyone?), but you'll have to put some effort into it and maybe buy some cookbooks. (Research shows this childhood habit theory is actually true for both food and money. Researchers at the University at Buffalo Jacobs School of Medicine and Biomedical Sciences have found that eating habits formed before age one often continue into childhood and even adulthood, as infants who got used to sweets and fatty foods continued to want them when they grew up. Likewise, the bank HSBC found that three in four "active savers," who are more likely to put money away for a rainy day, say that their parents taught them to save at a young age.)

With every paycheck you get, some portion of it should be going straight into short- and long-term savings. The precise portion will go up and down, depending on what else is going on in your life, but at least some chunk of change should be headed directly into the hot little hands of your future self—more on her in a minute.

Back before you were a mom (or mom-to-be if you are currently pregnant), your budget was probably a mishmash with around 35 percent going to housing, 20 percent to transportation, 15 percent to food, and the rest allocated between entertainment, health care, clothing, student loan and any other debt payments, and, lastly, savings.

When kids enter the picture, higher housing, food, and health care expenses start distorting that budget. Child care, or a drop in income if one person stays home, also claims more cash. Meanwhile, the pressure to save for the future is even more pressing. No wonder moms feel the financial strain. According to a

2015 Financial Finesse report on financial stress, the group facing the highest stress levels are low- and middle-income mothers. More than half of women between age 30 and 55 who have children under the age of 18 at home and earn $60,000 or less report high or overwhelming levels of stress. Even compared to dads earning similar amounts, moms are 40 percent more likely to report such high stress levels. (Not surprisingly, the group facing the lowest levels of financial stress were men over age 55 with no children at home and incomes over $100,000.)

It's not hard to see why kids can make such a mess of our financial lives. The U.S. Department of Agriculture estimates that babies cost the typical American family $12,940 each year. At the same time, finding a way to save is essential. You never know what's going to happen in the future: You (or your partner) could lose a job. A big unexpected cost, like a new refrigerator, could arise. An illness, or another pregnancy, could pop up.

Saving should feel as comforting as the luxury cashmere blanket that it is. If funneling money into your savings and investing accounts doesn't feel as satisfying as sliding your feet into fuzzy socks at the end of a long day, then it will be too tempting to find other uses for that money, like spending it on a new pair of (less comfortable but more stylish) shoes. If all your money is currently being claimed for other necessities, then it's time to take a closer look at what you can cut back (and we'll make that game plan together in the next section).

If you need some motivation to make those cutbacks, your new best friend, your future self, can help. It's time to get to know this lady you will one day become and to embrace and honor her. According to research by Hal Hershfield, an assistant professor in marketing at UCLA's Anderson School of Management, showing people aged photos of themselves increases the chances that they will save more money for the future. That's because people tend to feel disassociated from their future selves, almost like it is a stranger, he explains. But after looking at digitally altered photos of what they will look like in forty-plus years, they allocated twice as much money from a hypothetical windfall of $1,000 into long-term savings.

We can put these findings to use by getting to know our own future selves. You can start by downloading an aging app (many of which are available for free or for a nominal fee). I used Aging Booth, which turned my brown hair gray, thinned my lips, and filled by face with wrinkles. Only my eyes were recognizable, and it was terrifying. Barring tragedy, I will become that person—and I want her to be able to afford all the early bird specials she wants. You can age your partner, too, if you want some extra support on your new savings mission. (Just don't make the mistake I did and snap the pic while your loved one is sleeping and then share the disturbing pic after he wakes up. He might get mad.)

Fancy technology isn't the only way to get on a friendlier basis with this beautiful old lady (you). You can also write her a letter, have your eighty-year-old self write your present-day self a letter, spend more quality time with your grandmother, or volunteer in a nursing home. All will bring home the same point: That lady is going to need some money, even if it means some extra sacrifices today.

It's your job now to take care of her, just as you are taking care of your family today. Taking care of her will also help the financial stability of your family, who she won't need to rely on for financial aid because she'll be taking care of herself—and still hosting holiday dinners until she's ninety.

THE GAME PLAN

To ratchet up your savings to your target level, which should be between 10 percent to 15 percent for retirement savings and 5 percent to 10 percent for short-term savings, you can start by automating transfers into your savings accounts directly from your paycheck. (The earlier you start, the lower your target amount can be. The Center for Retirement Research at Boston College points out that if you start saving for retirement by age 25, then you can aim to save 10 percent a year to retire at age 65, but those who wait until age 35 should plan on 15 percent as an annual target.) Your bank probably offers the option of automatic transfers into a savings account for your short-term savings, and if you have the option of a 401(k) retirement account through your workplace, then you can set up the automated transfers there for your long-term retirement savings. To keep things simple, you can pick a target date fund for the year you'll likely retire, or you can pick a mix of the index funds and bond funds offered by your account provider. (The general wisdom is that you want to be more aggressive with your investments in your earlier years and then slowly get more conservative over time, but we'll dive into that much more deeply in Chapter 5, "Investing Mamas.")

It only gets harder to save once your children are born and as they get older, so this is something you want to start as soon as possible, like wearing sunscreen. If you're starting from a place of zero savings, then you can make it easier by moving slowly and starting by putting away just 2 percent a paycheck and then slowly raising that amount. If you are currently saving, just not quite enough, then take a close look at where you can cut back to make more room for savings. Likely targets include restaurant meals, personal care like hair salon appointments, clothing, and other more flexible expenses. (Don't get me wrong, self-care is important for moms, as we discussed, but that doesn't justify $200 highlights every other month, unless you're already reaching your savings targets.)

Research based on the spending patterns of 2,500 households from the RAND Corporation suggests that when people fear getting laid off, those flexible expenses are exactly where they cut back. They spend about 14 percent less on clothing, 11 percent less on dining out and other forms of entertainment, and 12 percent less on personal care splurges like haircuts and pedicures. Parents and soon-to-be parents can learn from that technique. While they might not fear a layoff, they are about to experience a different kind of financial shock, and one that also requires more savings. The researchers behind the study point out that making slow changes over time is far easier to handle than suddenly having to move to a smaller home because you can't pay your bills.

Food savings come largely from cooking at home more instead of dining out. Other savings come from paying for fewer movies and other forms of entertainment, personal care cutbacks, and fewer clothing purchases. Depending on your current spending habits, you might find room to cut back in different areas—for example, perhaps travel, Uber trips, or gym expenses are your weakness. Take a close look at what you discovered (in Chapter 1) about where your money is going so that you can figure out what to target. After tracking your spending for a month or closely reviewing your last monthly credit card bill, you can pick the areas that you're going to target so you can re-direct more money into savings.

Before we go further, we have to talk about debt—if you have any of it, especially high-interest-rate debt like credit card debt, then it's time to make a plan to pay it off, ASAP. Women are actually more likely than men to carry credit card debt; fewer than three in ten women say they always pay off their balance each month, according to a 2014 survey of over 1,000 American consumers by BMO Harris Bank. Most of us do have at least some amount of debt; it's often what got us where we are today, whether it helped fuel a degree or a car purchase or even a trip to the Bahamas. If you only have low-interest-rate student loan debt, then you can set that on the back burner while you con-tinue to make monthly payments, but any other kind of debt that is eating into your monthly budget needs to be unloaded faster than a recalled crib.

To tackle (and tame) this demon, first make a list of all the debt that you currently hold, along with the interest rate it car-ries. Rank the debts in order of highest interest rate debt first, to prioritize your payment schedule. If you have credit card debt, that's probably the most expensive one, with average interest rates around 17 percent, followed by car loans and any other kind of personal loan. Mortgages and student loans, depending on the type, can carry lower interest rates, and as long as you continue paying off the monthly payments to protect your credit score, there's not as great a rush to pay off the debts in full. When you're setting up your budget, you can redirect a portion of your monthly income toward your highest interest rate debts, until they're paid off in full. Paying off high interest is such a priority that you might want to consider taking more extreme short-term measures, like forgoing all new clothes or personal care appointments until the debt is paid off. (For extra help with the number crunching and to calculate how long it will take to fully unload a debt, you can try out the debt payoff calculators at Bankrate. com or CreditKarma.com.)

The wild card in these discussions is earnings—something that is almost always affected by motherhood, and a topic we will explore more deeply in the coming chapters. Whatever choices you make regarding your hours and career choices, we will get into the nitty-gritty of those choices in Chapter 4, "Like a Boss." One of the most important lessons to take from other moms is to wield your earning power and guard it as carefully as you do your body. It will always be there, even if you take a temporary break from the workforce or scale back your hours, ready for you to tap into and ramp up, according to your own needs and desires.

MONEY PLANNER

Staying organized, either through your own preferred paper filing system or with spreadsheets and online tools, and dedicating regular time every quarter to check in with your different financial accounts, review any outstanding to-dos, and adjust accounts and investments as necessary is one of the most wealth-producing habits you can adopt. In fact, as my sister Christina got ready to graduate from medical school and prepare for her new life as a working professional, that was my main message to her: Get a binder.

My sister had paperwork for accounts for student loans, retirement savings, short-term savings, credit cards, and all kinds of other papers scattered about. With all that clutter staring her in the face, she could hardly even begin to make big decisions, like how much to put into her retirement account. She couldn't tell when her health insurance was expiring or what her workplace benefits were because finding that information first required sorting through dozens of papers. I suggested that she either put everything into an organized binder or switch to an online system like Mint (my preferred choice, simply to put an end to all the paperwork) that would help her track documents and save everything in one place. After that was taken care of, she could turn to the bigger decisions about retirement savings and investments.

Getting organized can also help with that other skill we need to cultivate as early as possible: comfort (and confidence) with managing money. That's a tough one, because in some ways, by the time we realize that we want to feel comfortable about money, so much has already been set into motion: Our attitudes and habits about money and our spending and saving tendencies are often already established. Those patterns (which often come from our families) can be changed, but first we have to recognize what they are, like Alison Singh Gee did.

Alison sat down with her husband, Ajay, and talked about their earliest money memories, an idea she got from a financial self-help book. "Suze Orman suggested writing down your first-ever memory of money. It was the most important exercise I ever did," she says. Her husband realized that he got his "money makes you evil" attitude from getting falsely accused of stealing when he was young. Alison remembered around age six having lunch with her father, younger brother, and grandfather, when her father suddenly erupted in rage, almost turning over the table. Her grandfather, a successful businessman, had just said that he would only leave an inheritance to his male heirs and not his granddaughters.

That experience led Alison to decide she was never going to give money such power over her. She was going to be above it. She was certainly not going to actively manage her money, because that is what she thought mean people did, and it could lead to explosive family fights like the one she witnessed as a six-year-old. Once she recognized those deeply rooted money lessons she had absorbed at such a young age, she could start to move past them. Only then did she realize that managing her money was a healthy thing to embrace.

Talking directly to the older women in your family, including your grandmother and mother, about money can also help you move past any discomfort you have about the topic and embrace your new role as chief financial officer of your life (and CFO of your family). When I called my eighty-nine-year-old grandmother at her retirement community in New Jersey to interview her about her financial life, I learned some surprising things, all of which shed light on the frugality that my own mom has always demonstrated to me: When my grandmother became a mom at age 22, she barely had the money to go out to dinner to celebrate her wedding anniversary. And that was back when babysitters cost 50 cents an hour and a three-course meal at a nice restaurant was under $5. My grandfather's job provided a comfortable (though not lavish) lifestyle for the family with five children, but she wasn't able to feel financially secure or to save money until she went back to work at age 41. She became a real estate agent when her youngest child went to school. Much of her savings today come from stocks that her grandfather left to her in his will over fifty years ago, which she never sold. (She's also taught me countless other financial lessons over the years through less formal conversations: Be frugal, but you can never have too many nice diamond rings. Have your own money, even when you're married. Get a prenup before a later-in-life marriage. Don't give away milk for free or no one will buy the cow . . . but that's a topic for a different book.)

When you're comfortable talking and thinking about your money, then it's easier to share the job with a partner, too, as well as notice potential red flags in potential partners, from overspending to secretiveness about money. If you've already been making decisions about investments, insurance policies, and savings accounts on your own, then it will be a smooth transition to continue doing so as part of a couple. Research suggests that not only do couples report feeling happier when they manage their money together, but they also make better financial decisions. In fact, a 2014 study from UBS Wealth Management of over 2,500 high-net-worth investors found that couples who shared their financial management tasks reported the highest levels of satisfaction and confidence about their money and that they also had fewer disagreements about money. (Despite the rewards, just one in four couples reported managing money this way.) Also, given the high likelihood that at some point women will be widowed, divorced, or managing money on their own for another reason, it pays—literally—to always play a leading role when it comes to your finances. At some point, you probably won't have a choice in the matter.

SMART MOM, RICH MOM
ACTION STEPS

1. Review your current spending patterns and check in with your current savings rate; figure out what you can cut back to reach your target savings goals. It might require making some tough decisions (cable TV or a savings account?), but they will force you to consider your priorities. (If you have a partner, then you can do this together over a money date.)

2. Identify your current short-term and long-term savings goals. Do you know what you're working toward? Spelling it out helps provide the motivation needed to get there.

3. Cultivate feelings of gratitude and abundance every day. Take a moment to appreciate the material and nonmaterial gifts in your life.

4. Age your face and spend some time with your older self. You can do this with an app like AgingBooth or online—a web search of "aging face websites" will bring up the latest tools available.

5. Call an older woman in your family to talk about her life's money lessons. Ask her questions about tough financial times she experienced, money regrets, what she did right, and how she learned her own spending and saving habits.

6. Reflect on your own feelings about managing money and what early money experiences might be influencing them. Do you remember how your parents discussed money in front of you growing up?

7. Embrace your role as chief financial officer of your life by setting aside time every few months to review your current financial accounts, your long- and short-term goals, and the steps you need to take. Develop your system for tracking and storing financial paperwork.

3

TIMING
IS EVERYTHING

I f you are a mom, then you've probably noticed that having babies is pretty expensive. Babies born today cost the average American family about a quarter of a million dollars before they turn eighteen, and that figure doesn't even include college tuition. After considering inflation, we spend about 22 percent more on our children than our grandparents did, thanks largely to the cost of child care and higher standards for everything from food to clothing to activities.

For many women, the costliest part of having babies is the impact on our earnings—even if we stay in the workforce in some capacity, we might scale back our hours, get passed over for promotions (or opt out of them), or choose a more flexible but less lucrative career path. In fact, research suggests that having children improves men's income while depressing women's income, even after controlling for hours worked. The reason seems to be most closely tied to employers' assumption that mothers do not deserve as high a salary as a father doing the same job. (These findings, published by sociologists Michelle Budig and Paula England, are strongest among women in lower-income jobs and weakest among high-earning women.)

When we have our babies can also have a big impact on our wealth levels, and smart moms often become moms when it is least disruptive to their careers and earning power, to the extent that they can control it. Of course, babies are often unexpected, or long sought after, and we might have little control over the timing of their arrival. But that doesn't mean we can't prepare for parenthood and make the best financial choices possible for our families based on whatever stage we're at.

If you are still in the planning stages of parenthood (or want to grow your family further), then you might be able to use some of the latest research on the so-called motherhood penalty to your benefit. Research shows that in general the longer women wait to have kids, the less of a negative impact it has on their income. Amalia Miller, a University of Virginia economist, has found that each year a woman in her twenties or early thirties waits to have children can increase her earnings by almost 10 percent. Women with college degrees in professional and managerial positions enjoyed the largest financial benefit to waiting.

At the same time, other research suggests that having babies relatively early, while still in your twenties, can be a good career move, especially for women in training-heavy fields like law, medicine, or academia. That way, you're juggling child care for very young children while you are still studying but before larger (and frequently less flexible) responsibilities of real work begin.

In their book *Mothers on the Fast Track,* coauthors (and mother-daughter team) Mary Ann Mason and Eve Mason Eckman write that because careers peak in intensity for many professionals during their thirties, thirtysomething parents with children who are already beyond their baby years can often get ahead more easily. They call that decade between ages 20 and 30 the "make or break" years, when it's hardest, and most stressful, to have young children and babies.

One of the most successful moms I know, Lindsay Kelly, one of the lawyers I mentioned in Chapter 2, started having children in her mid-twenties, and she says that's what allowed her to thrive professionally during her thirties. She was done taking maternity leaves and ready to take on more professional responsibility while her kids started elementary school, just as some of her colleagues were starting their families.

Similarly, my friend Alison, who has a PhD in health economics and is quickly ascending the ranks as an international consultant, also started her family while she was still in school. Now that she is at a manager level and her two sons are past the baby stage, she is more easily able to consider international assignments and heftier management duties. Both of these women are highly educated professionals and able to be the breadwinners for their families partly because of how they timed their family planning. As the research shows, that ideal timing depends on many factors and can vary greatly from one mama to the next. The best we can do for ourselves and our families is to make informed decisions and deal with the results as best we can.

FINANCIAL PREP WORK

Regardless of where you fall on the timing or earnings spectrum, there are plenty of ways to keep costs under control so that you don't do damage to your long-term saving and investing goals. While trimming a few bucks off each diaper purchase by signing up for Amazon discounts or buying used clothes won't make you a millionaire, they are smart habits for moms of all income levels to employ. Cooking basic meals at home instead of eating out, sharing bedrooms at a young age, and skipping most of the items on the shopping lists suggested by retailers pushing baby products are all good places to start, too. Babies don't really need wipes warmers, especially if you have a hair dryer nearby! And even though the toddler selection of laptops rivals that of their grown-up counterparts, you actually don't need to buy your little one the latest kid-friendly tablet each year. (They'll stay busy enough stealing yours.)

The biggest takeaway from my interviews with moms is to find a way to continue saving and investing despite the increased pressure on your budget. One of the best ways for expectant parents to prepare for affording a baby is to practice living off of only one income and saving the second one (for those with partners) or saving for the expected cost of child care, which averages about $1,200 a month but can be higher in urban areas, while you're still pregnant. That way, you'll get in the habit of living off of your new and reduced budget while also building up a nest egg to help fund those first-year costs.

SEVEN WAYS NEW PARENTS CAN CUT COSTS

❑ Sign up for any available flex-spending programs through your workplace for child care expenses, health care expenses, and commuting costs.

❑ Develop some easy-to-make, family-friendly meals that everyone enjoys. If you need inspiration, check out the websites of kid-friendly cookbook authors, like Weelicious.com.

❑ Review your current health insurance and make sure you've selected the optimal type available for your family; you can typically make adjustments during the next open enrollment period or following the birth of a child (as well as other major life events, like marriage).

❑ Research, compare prices, and save for any big child-related expenses, including cars, cribs, and even homes, if you plan to move soon.

❑ Ask family and friends for hand-me-downs for clothing, furniture, and toys. (For safety, always make sure used items haven't been recalled by checking at www.Recalls.gov and buy new car seats with the latest safety upgrades.)

❑ Stick with gender-neutral colors to increase the chances you can reuse items for any future children (or resell the items when you're done with them).

❑ Gently encourage parents and relatives to direct their generosity at gift-giving occasions toward big-ticket items you really need or by contributing to your child's 529 college savings account.

Regardless of how old your children are, you can get started now and catch up quickly by trimming the more flexible parts of your budget (food, entertainment, personal care), as discussed in Chapter 2, and redirecting that money into savings and investing accounts. Even with endless prep work under your belt, though, few mamas feel completely financially prepared for the shock of being responsible for a new baby. When I first visited Beth and Sean Moynihan on a rainy Sunday at their Baltimore townhome as they were weeks away from the arrival of their daughter Abigail, they were still unpacking boxes in her freshly painted pale green nursery. Sean, a mechanical engineer, guessed that they had spent close to $6,000 on the crib, blankets, bouncy seats, and other gear. Beth, a nurse, was also thinking hard about how to handle the coming child care costs through a mix of a local co-op arrangements with her coworkers as well as help from nearby family members.

To help with those upcoming expenses, Beth and Sean cut back on their traveling and entertainment expenses and asked their parents to start contributing money to a college savings account at future birthdays and Christmases. "We started talking about cutting back on vacations, traveling, and going out. . . . Then we can have more money for the baby's needs now," Beth told me.

Fast-forward four years later: Beth and Sean, who are both in their early thirties, have a second daughter, Claire, and bought a home in Northern Virginia. Beth is working part-time as a nurse practitioner at a local hospital and her daughters attend school and day care. While still making money-savvy choices, Beth is finding it harder than ever to save. She told me that she continues to encourage her family members to put money into college savings accounts, but as her daughters get older, they also want presents to open. "We've fallen a little behind where we thought we'd be, because our child care costs went up, and with me not working full-time, [savings] had to take a backseat. Once I go back to work full-time and our daughters are in public elementary school, we'll be able to save what we're paying in child care now—so we had to readjust our thinking," she explains. She and Sean still keep their own travel and entertainment costs down, opting for at-home date nights over wine and a movie instead of going to restaurants for a meal and drinks. It's a solid long-term strategy that doesn't require too much sacrifice today.

Like Beth and Sean, most parents don't time conception directly to their bank account levels, but money often plays a background role in the decision. When the Pew Research Center asked prospective parents what would make them decide to have a child, the most highly cited response, after finding the right partner, was having adequate financial resources. When Pew asked mothers age 50 and older why they opted to have no more children, the most common answer, after wanting to have more time for existing children, was the cost. (Moms were actually more likely to cite cost as a factor in limiting family size than fathers.) Pew has also found that among millennials who are now in their twenties and early thirties—prime childbearing years—the feeling of not being financially ready is delaying parenthood. Around 22 percent said they delayed having a baby because of the economy.

Whether you already have two spaghetti-covered mouths to feed or you're approaching your first delivery day, you've probably noticed that you can't exactly put your children on pause until you've saved up some more cash for their expenses. You can, however, shape some family spending habits so that supporting your family doesn't feel like a bomb went off in your bank account. Instead, it can feel more like a slow leak—but one that's watering a beautiful garden.

READY TO EXPAND

Adding another person to the family is usually not quite as expensive as the first, and in fact, additional costs tend to lessen with each additional child. The USDA found that parents spend less per child the more children they have, as a result of shared bedrooms, clothing, toys, and even sibling discounts at schools or child care centers. Parents can also spend less on food per child when cooking for multiple little ones.

You can leverage these savings further by being smart about your purchases, like sticking with gender-neutral items so that your second (or third) child can wear the same winter jacket or summer floatie as his or her big brother or sister. You can also have siblings share rooms instead of moving into a bigger home when a new baby comes home. Jennifer Saranow Schultz, a mom of two and blogger behind the HintMama.com website, which offers daily savings tips for moms, recommends looking for adaptable baby gear, like strollers that easily convert from single to double strollers, video monitors that let you add multiple cameras, and toys and books that appeal to both genders. When her son joined the family a couple years after her daughter, she drastically reduced her costs by reusing her daughter's stroller, car seat, changing table, bouncy seat, and swing. As long as these products haven't been recalled (or, in the case of car seats, expired) and you know they've been taken care of, then reusing those big-ticket items poses no added risk.

Jennifer is also reusing her daughter's gender-neutral clothes, burp cloths, breast pump accessories, and bottles (with new nipples). She teamed up with a local friend who has a two-year-old boy and infant daughter—they trade clothes so that their newborns have plenty of gender-appropriate gear. Going forward, she's paying even more attention to buying gender-neutral items, so her son can one day wear his sister's green Crocs or ride her red scooter. She also plans to have her son and daughter share a room, as soon as he can sleep through the night.

Molly Thornberg, founder of the Digital Mom blog, found that by the time her fourth child was born, she had learned her lesson about overspending. She and her husband realized that their newborn wouldn't actually wear baby shoes and he wouldn't really care if he had designer sheets or not. She had also learned to stop buying items that didn't even exist when she was growing up, including battery-operated nasal aspirators and Diaper Genies. She also adopted certain tricks like bulk-buying diapers from Amazon and borrowing secondhand gear like bouncy chairs from friends. Her fourth baby's entire nursery was finished for under $500, she says, which is almost what she spent on her first baby's bedding alone.

Even if your future children aren't here yet, it can pay to plan ahead, especially before making any big purchases. I will always be grateful to Jane, our real estate agent (and mom of three), who gently discouraged us from buying a two-bedroom condo that caught our eye shortly after our daughter was born. We were living in a one-bedroom apartment at the time and were desperate to get some more space and our own washing machine and dryer. I was ready to stop carting our laundry up and down five stories with a baby attached to me in a carrier, especially during those days of endless newborn washing.

When we found a nice two-bedroom condo for sale and wanted to make an offer, Jane reminded us, "Even if you can't imagine it now, families have a way of expanding." Of course, she was right. We kept looking and finally purchased a three-bedroom house that left us with room to grow. A few years later, when our son was born, we were glad we didn't have to move again (and pay all the related costs). Thanks to Jane's advice, we had plenty of space for our new baby.

With housing typically accounting for a full 30 percent of child-related expenses, it's a good subject to get creative about. A growing number of families are even opting for a multigenerational housing solution and living under the same roof with grandparents, who might also be able to assist with child care. In the course of my research, I met a single mom who opted to move back home with her own parents while raising her young children and married couples who invited their parents to move into an extra bedroom.

That was the case for Katy Hewson and her husband, Keith, who were newlyweds when I first spoke with them in 2009. They were living with her parents in a three-bedroom townhome in Houston. The arrangement might sound unusual, but it worked well for both couples. They each saved thousands of dollars on housing costs, and Katy, a social worker, and Keith, an airline pilot, paid off their student loans while building up a nest egg. They also seemed to truly enjoy living together. Keith often traveled for days or even weeks at a time for his job, and Katy's parents kept her company.

After their first son was born, Keith and Katy continued living with her parents, saving money and taking advantage of the child care help. Those savings gave them the nest egg that let them move into a larger home in the suburbs of Houston when their second son arrived. Today, Keith and Katy, who are in their mid-thirties, live in League City, where they have plenty of green space for their sons, ages five and two, to run around.

Katy's parents are still nearby and babysit at least a few times a month, which she estimates saves her close to $1,500 a year— and an immeasurable amount of peace of mind knowing that they can come over quickly if needed. "If I want to stay after work for a work function or go out with girlfriends who live in town, I can ask my parents to go pick the kids up or have them go to their house after school," she says. "They're always available to help us."

She and Keith also escape for weeklong getaways to places like Napa Valley and Cancun, leaving their children home with Katy's parents. "That right there is invaluable," she says.

The best part, of course, isn't about the money. "The best part is that my kids have such a great relationship with my parents," she says. Her kids also get a more relaxed mom, who knows an extra pair of hands (or two) are just a call away if the normal routine gets derailed with work responsibilities or sickness. That's the kind of help that can really keep a mom sane and relaxed—and gainfully employed.

SMART MOM, RICH MOM
ACTION STEPS

1. Get a handle on your current and expected child-related costs by estimating how much you spend (or will spend) on housing, child care and education, food, transportation, health care, clothing, and other extras because of your children. Are there places you could spend less—for example, by cooking at home more or accepting more hand-me-down clothing from friends and family?

2. Save on everyday items by reusing toys and clothes, sharing bedrooms, or taking advantage of sibling discounts at child care facilities. Buy gender-neutral items to make this easier if you plan on having more children.

3. Look for ways to enlist the help of family and friends, especially any nearby grandparents. If they are willing and able to babysit, even on occasion, it can save you money and reduce stress.

4. If you're still growing your family, consider the timing of births relative to your expected fertility and career plans. While it's often beyond our control, timing can have a big impact on future earning potential and, as a result, your family's financial security.

5. Consider whether you are paying a "motherhood penalty"—are your wages suffering as a result of discrimination against moms? If so, consider advocating for a raise or looking for a new job.

4

LIKE A BOSS

When I brought my tiny, six-pound newborn home from the hospital for the first time, I was so overwhelmed by the task of taking care of her that I could barely find time to eat. Between trying to get the hang of breast feeding, changing her diapers, and recovering from a C-section after a forty-eight-hour labor, I was utterly exhausted. And the immense responsibility and love that I felt for this tiny life was exploding inside me in a hormone-fueled volcano.

At the same time, I felt more vulnerable than ever, too. Physically, I was weaker than usual, since I was still recovering from the birth, and for the first time in my marriage, I was completely dependent on my husband for support—physical, emotional, and financial. I was at the beginning of my four-and-a-half month, mostly unpaid, maternity leave.

As I gazed at my daughter's thick, dark hair and creamy skin, I started daydreaming about how I could take back control of this disorienting situation. I would have to wait for my body to heal and the postpartum hormones to pass through my system, but I could start planning for how to take control over my financial life. Maybe becoming a mom didn't have to mean that I had to stop earning money entirely, even temporarily. I certainly felt more motivated than ever to provide for my new family, given our skyrocketing costs.

Armed with the conviction that it was my job to make sure we kept this little nugget well fed and cared for, as well as the desire to prove to myself that my ambition hadn't been destroyed along with my stomach muscles, I picked up a couple freelance assignments while on maternity leave. I interviewed experts and typed up my articles while my newborn napped in her car seat next to my feet by my desk. I started dreaming up what would eventually become my Etsy shop of money planners, digital workbooks that help people manage their finances. Little by little, I felt like I was taking back control over our lives.

Other mothers have described similar moments of clarity, when they realized that becoming a mom also meant they wanted to shore up their earning power. Farnoosh Torabi, a money expert and TV personality, says it was her newborn son that made her want to launch her own podcast, so she could guarantee herself an income stream, regardless of what her employers or the economy were doing. She wrote about this epiphany on her blog, dubbing it the Baby Effect: "I'm talking about staring at your baby and realizing, 'I can't have any more financial uncertainty. I can't afford to have a slow year—ever.'"

That rush of motivation to earn more money can hit new moms hard—and it can be difficult to balance with the simultaneous duties of taking care of a baby. It can also be hard when you're fighting against the "motherhood penalty" at work that we discussed in Chapter 3. Employers often pay moms less because of the perception, or reality, that they are working fewer hours. The good news is that one of the central guiding principles of smart moms—to always be earning money, even if it's in a reduced capacity—doesn't have to mean working ten-hour days when you have a newborn at home or always missing your elementary schooler's soccer games. While plenty of smart moms follow a traditional career route, climbing corporate ladders in a Sheryl Sandberg–type fashion, it is hardly the only way. Many successful moms I talked to designed their own, less linear career paths, and those paths let them grow their incomes while also being the kind of moms they wanted to be.

THE STRAIGHT AND NARROW

When I started looking for moms to interview who followed a traditional full-time worker path, filled with at least eight to nine hours of face time in the office, each day, along with requirements that prohibit telecommuting or flexible scheduling, I was hard-pressed to find them. Almost every professional woman I reached out to explained that her schedule allowed for at least some degree of flexibility, to take sick children to a pediatrician or to attend school functions on occasion. My sister, a doctor specializing in family medicine who works full-time, arranged her schedule so that she worked Tuesday through Friday and could be home on Mondays. Full-time lawyers and government employees explained similar flex schedules that let them be home in time for day care pickup or let them pick one day a week to work at home. (Women working low-wage jobs tell a very different story, and those challenges deserve their own book.)

The ability to negotiate some degree of flexibility even in full-time, demanding jobs is a relatively new phenomenon. Even our mother's generation, just thirty years ago, felt more stigmatized and less able to ask for the flexibility they so desperately needed. Part of that shift comes from the incredible growth of workers who are caring for either young children or aging adults. According to research conducted at the University of Rhode Island, one in three workers are currently caring for an older adult while 43 percent care for children (12 percent of those surveyed juggled both responsibilities). National studies conducted by the Family and Work Institute reveal similar figures, and with the population of elderly in the United States set to double in the next thirty years, the percentage of workers moonlighting as caregivers will likely skyrocket. As a result, acceptance of the need for flexibility, which is crucial to caregivers of both young children and older adults, appears poised to continue to spread. When your boss also has to hurry home to care for her aging mother, she's more likely to understand why you need to do the same when your baby gets a cold.

The fact is, there are some weeks when being a parent simply demands that kind of flexibility. I am typing this from home while my son naps upstairs, after getting a call from day care to pick him up early because he might have pinkeye. That means I'll have to take him to the doctor in the morning and keep him home tomorrow while he might be contagious. Meanwhile, I need to leave work early later in the week, too, because of a scheduled dental appointment for my daughter. Sometimes I feel like I never have a "typical" week, when I am actually sitting at my desk from nine to five, because of all of these demands, both scheduled and unexpected, and I am grateful that my boss—a mom herself—allows that kind of flexibility.

The need for workplace flexibility is so widely acknowledged that in the summer of 2014, the White House held a summit on working families where experts, corporate leaders, and politicians gathered to discuss how to make it easier for those in the midst of that juggle. On one high-powered panel, Bob Moritz, chairman of the accounting firm PricewaterhouseCoopers, encouraged his fellow corporate leaders to embrace the business case for flexibility. Engaging your workforce, he says, depends on allowing them to take care of their home responsibilities. "If you're engaging them, you're going to get 75 percent more productivity," he said.

As proof, he explained that after PwC changed its policy several years ago to allow workers to take unlimited paid sick leave, the number of sick days taken across the company went down, not up. "You actually got more productivity," he told the rapt audience. The real clincher is that the updated sick leave policy also specified that it could be taken not just when employees themselves are sick, but when they need to take care of kids or older adults.

That is exactly what many working parents say they need—the ability to take time off during the workday without being penalized for it. The Family and Work Institute finds that most employers now offer at least some degree of flexibility. Eight in ten employers with at least fifty employees say they allow people to take time off for family or personal reasons without losing pay or sometimes change their start or stopping times for the day.

Still, it's hard to be a working mama (or papa). I felt like I was failing at it even as I was covering the White House Summit on Working Families. The event required pre-security screening, since the president would be there, so I arrived as early as I could after dropping off my two children at school. It was too late for access to the main auditorium, so I was shunted off to a press room where the speakers were on a video feed. Michelle Obama, the star of the event, did not start speaking until after I was due at school pickup at 5:30. And the preconference phone call with White House senior adviser Valerie Jarrett occurred at 4:30 p.m. on Sunday, when I was at my daughter's swimming lesson and playing with my son in the baby pool. There was simply no way to do it all.

Even with a supportive employer, it is hard to leave at five o'clock every day and walk past rows of childless twentysomethings (and older managers with independent kids or stay-at-home partners), knowing they will keep their eyes glued to their computer screens for another couple hours at least. Even with a comfortable lactation room nearby, it's challenging to leave your desk to pump twice a day. Putting in eight hours—or more—on four hours of interrupted sleep (thanks to a teething toddler) will never be easy. Responding to client requests through a weekend or working until 10 p.m. on a deadline instead of being home for bedtime is painful. For some mothers, those kinds of sacrifices will be unacceptable, and they will decide to leave the workforce as a result—or get pushed out after finding themselves lacking the support they need to be a working parent.

Still, lots of moms find ways to make full-time work bearable and even enjoyable. Here are some of the strategies that emerged from our conversations:

- Choose a job and field you love, so you are eager to get back to work, even when stressed out by motherhood. It's easier to go back to work when you're exhausted when you actually enjoy it. Sitting down at your work computer with coffee on a Monday morning after a chaotic family weekend can be downright pleasurable.
- Go into a field that allows you to support your family. It's hard to justify (and afford) continuing to work if your salary does not pay the day care bills. Women who get degrees that allow them to enter higher-paying fields have more financial power and flexibility to pay for reputable, licensed child care that they feel comfortable with.
- Ask for the flexibility you need. If you believe your work life would be significantly improved by working at home on Wednesdays, then ask for that. If you need to leave at 3 p.m. on Thursdays to take your daughter to dance class, then make the request.
- Negotiate flexibility during the job offer process. Once you receive a job offer, it's your turn to negotiate. In addition to pay, consider asking for other flexibility perks that would help, such as the ability to work from home or adopt a flexible daily schedule (working 7 a.m. to 3 p.m., for example) so that you can get your kids to and from school.

- Switch jobs if it's not working. Sometimes a job is just not a good fit for the lifestyle you want, and it's okay to acknowledge that and move on.
- Take full advantage of the benefits available. If your workplace offers maternity leave beyond the twelve weeks required by the Family and Medical Leave Act, then consider taking it. If your corporate culture allows for telecommuting or other flexibilities, then take advantage of them.
- Perfect the art of sending simple notes about whereabouts. If your child has to go to the pediatrician or you need to leave early for a ballet performance, there is no need to send a long, guilt-laden email to your supervisor and coworkers. Instead, opt for simple informative notes: "I will be out of the office starting at 3 p.m. today to attend a school event and I'll be back online afterward." Coworkers don't need or want to hear about the rash on your toddler's stomach or how his cough sounded at 5 a.m.
- Work out fair deals with your partner. The moms I interviewed tended to share duties with their partners so they are not the only ones having to handle pediatrician visits, mealtimes, and school visits.
- Refuse to feel guilty. You might be walking out at 5 p.m., but the coworkers you are leaving behind staring at their screens might be watching YouTube videos or daydreaming about happy hour. Guilt can interfere with productivity, so make a conscious effort to refuse to feel it, at home or at work.

- Get paid what you deserve. Even if you leave early and take advantage of other flexibilities, you still deserve to get paid well for what you do. Don't let your working mom status trick you into thinking you don't deserve raises and promotions.

- Use (and limit) tech. Your smartphone can help you respond to work emails in between your bedtime routine, but it can also make that routine take twice as long if your children sense you aren't present, so put the phone down and turn it off when possible.

- Enlist help. Whether in the form of grandparents, paid caregivers, housecleaners, grocery delivery, or other services, smart moms know how to ask for help. Paying for time-saving services can help them focus on the more important tasks at hand, like spending time with their children. They also feel supported by their larger communities, including close girlfriends and especially other mothers who understand and relate to their challenges and offer encouragement and camaraderie. When you are struggling to lead a presentation after two hours of sleep because your daughter has a cough and you just got an email from day care alerting you to a lice outbreak, it's a little easier to deal with the chaos if you can text your girlfriend to commiserate and she immediately texts back telling you that you will get through it—and that her son threw up all night.

The good news, too, is that future moms are poised to have an easier time, as younger workers demand greater flexibility, often before they have kids. In addition to its sick leave policy, PwC also launched a program that lets interested employees work just a few months a year, during the firm's busiest season. It's a version of part-time work that leaves plenty of time for uninterrupted focus on other pursuits, including children, during the rest of the year. While plenty of parents and older workers take advantage of the policy, it gets much of its support from an unlikely group: millennials at the beginning of their careers. PwC found that young workers in their twenties were especially eager for flexibility, not so they could care for children but to pursue outside interests, from traveling to skiing to running a small business. As they get older and have children, the ones who become moms and dads will shift to parenting in their off-hours, using the flexibility they've already established.

A DIFFERENT PATH

A traditional, linear trajectory is not the career path for everyone, and many moms reject it. They might temporarily scale back their work while their children are young, accepting part-time gigs or freelance work, and then ease their way back into more responsibility when they're ready.

Instead of logging at least forty hours a week, their schedules might look more like that of Christine Ryan Jyoti, a mom in the Washington, D.C., area who decided not to return to her full-time job as communications director for a nonprofit after she had her now school-age daughter and son. Returning to work just felt like too much to juggle with her growing family.

But she knew she wanted to keep working in some capacity, particularly by writing, something she'd always enjoyed and felt good at. So Christine started picking up freelance assignments for a financial website, which soon upgraded her to a position as regular contributor, and she began earning her first steady paycheck in four years. Her job now takes up about ten to fifteen hours a week and she earns a steady stream of income—not as much as her former full-time job paid, but enough to keep her feeling on top of her financial game. "Freelance writing fits my life," she says, and the work keeps her resume up to date in case she one day decides to return to an office job. She's also starting yoga teacher training to explore different directions for her career in a way that continues to allow her to be at home after school for her children, too.

That patchwork approach is increasingly popular for a segment of educated, professional women—the same women who, two decades ago, might have dropped out of the workforce altogether. Pamela Stone, professor of sociology at Hunter College in New York, who has long studied women who "opt out," and Meg Clare Lovejoy, a visiting assistant professor at Augustana College in Illinois, found that among a group of thirty educated, professional women who left their full-time jobs when their children were young, two-thirds of them had returned to some type of employment within ten years.

Like Christine, though, the work was not like the demanding, highly paid jobs they held before. Instead, the women in their study had embraced lower-paying but more flexible roles, often in the field of education, including teaching, career counseling, and fundraising. Many of them had taken on project-based work that allowed them control over the hours. For moms who want to be home at 3 p.m. when school gets out, that kind of flexibility can make a big difference.

Smart moms, it turns out, seek to maximize not just their paycheck, but their career satisfaction—which over the long run can end up helping your earnings, too, because you stay in the workforce longer. That's why sometimes even strategic pay cuts can pay off in the long run if they allow you to continue working when you might have otherwise felt forced to stop. (The moms who do stop working are usually at either end of the spectrum: They earn so little that they can't afford to pay for child care, or their household income is so high that they can easily afford to drop their paycheck, Pew reports.)

This concept is so prevalent that academics have generated a name for it: the kaleidoscope career. Professors Lisa Mainiero and Sherry Sullivan coined the term in the mid-2000s after studying shifting workplace patterns among professionals. They found that women often followed what they dubbed a "beta" career path, which focuses first on challenge, then balance, and finally authenticity. In contrast, they found men follow an "alpha" career pattern that seeks balance only at the end of one's career and an unfettered drive for challenge and climbing the traditional career ladder earlier on.

Jamie Ladge, a professor at Northeastern University, has similarly found that parents who go part-time for a period can feel just as fulfilled in their work lives as those who continue working full-time. The personal satisfaction that people feel from their careers has more to do with their own feelings about their work than the amount on their paycheck, she found.

Many women, in other words, aren't solely focused on getting ahead and ticking off external measures of success: a larger salary, a more important title, a bigger office. They place a lot of value on having a job that reflects their values, including the importance of handling their family responsibilities. And they consciously opt out of that traditional career ladder in favor of a more customized path that feels right to them.

Passages author Gail Sheehy (featured in Chapter 2), embodies this approach. From her days as a single working mom to a successful author, she has always kept working amid her caregiving responsibilities. When her husband, the editor Clay Felker, got sick with cancer at the end of his life, she had to once again juggle her work responsibilities with taking care of someone else. While she had to scale back her work, she made sure to continue earning income so that she could both afford to take care of her and her ailing husband, but also so that she could still retain her own identity.

Sheehy says:

Men and women give up their jobs and stop working because it's just too much, but I knew that was a dead end…. If you give up your identity, once the role of caregiver ends, as it inevitably does, who are you? It's very difficult to get back in the game, not just as a writer but in any field. I always advise people to keep your hand in no matter what you do, even if you have to support people to help you so you can continue to do some work. It keeps you going so when the caregiving vigil is over, you have a life you can pick back up.

She takes on more or less freelance work, teaching projects, and book contracts depending on how much time and energy she has needed to devote to caring for others at different points in her life.

Once again, it's not just moms who make this choice, either. In her PhD research at Purdue University, Elizabeth Wilhoit has found that women without children are also often eager to leave their traditional, full-time jobs because they conflict with their personal or professional goals. The masculine, linear model of professional success does not resonate with many women, she says, because they seek authenticity—jobs that reflect their values and identity. Moms might have invented the kaleidoscope career out of necessity, but other people increasingly see its appeal, too—and its growing prevalence makes it easier for all of us to negotiate flexibility into our work.

Mainiero and Sullivan have also noted that young men, and millennials in general, are more likely to prioritize balance, even early in their careers. Mainiero told me that her students often say that instead of working for a big financial firm in Manhattan after graduation, they want to have a more balanced life instead.

The moms who thrive on a more winding career path shared these strategies for success:

- Keep working in some capacity, even during the most challenging years, when you are sleep deprived, juggling multiple children under the age of five, and stressed to your limits. If you temporarily opt out of full-time work, you can still maintain your social media accounts and professional identities, contacts, networks, and skills by taking on short-term assignments. Moms who don't do this put their future earning potential at risk. Even mothers who adopt the identity of a stay-at-home mom often find some way to stay in the professional game, by blogging, coaching, volunteering, and attending conferences in their field.

- Think like an entrepreneur. Whether it's building their brands on Twitter and LinkedIn, to maintain a presence and contacts even when scaling back on full-time work, or picking up side gigs to supplement their income, moms who embrace nontraditional career paths are always hustling. They are looking out for their next opportunity and attracting new prospects into their lives by making themselves known for the skills and expertise that they enjoy.

- Say yes to the right opportunities. In the study by Pamela Stone and Meg Clare Lovejoy, many of the women who found their way back to employment after a break happened upon their next career opportunities almost by accident. They didn't go out and apply for job openings or send their resumes around; instead, former contacts and people within their networks who knew of their skill set asked them if they would be interested in their new positions.

- Think long term. Child care expenses are highest before children start kindergarten, and moms (and dads) often feel like the entirety of their paycheck is going toward paying someone else to hang out with their children. But over time, those child care costs go down and income grows, which makes those crunched years worth the struggle.

- Always have a Plan B in place. Jobs can suddenly disappear or become incompatible with family life, or a primary breadwinner can suddenly become unable to work. Smart moms are ready to adapt by having their backup plans in mind. That might mean having a hefty savings account ready to get you through a few years of much lower household income, a side business of contract or freelance work that you can ramp up, or a business plan for a consulting service based on your professional expertise. (My book *The Economy of You* explains how to launch this kind of flexible side business.)
- Know that sometimes strategic pay cuts can make sense. Sometimes, accepting a lower-paying job or even declining a promotion that would require more travel and management duties can be the right choice over the long term, because it increases the chances that you'll stay in the workforce—and keep earning.
- Be open to reinventing yourself and making different choices. Smart moms know that the workforce, and their families, are constantly changing, which means the amount and type of work they want to do is changing, too. They constantly check in with themselves (and their families) and make adjustments.
- Take advantage of working parent-friendly tax

benefits. From IRAs for retirement to pretax flex-spending accounts that can help reduce the cost of child care, smart moms take advantage of them all, to make sure they are keeping as much money in their families as possible. If you're not sure about the programs currently available to you, ask your human resources contact at work (or your partner's work) for a list of benefits.

THE DIY METHOD

For some mothers, that design-your-own path includes self-employment, either by choice or because they find that their traditional jobs simply do not mesh with motherhood in a satisfying way. For Jordan Lloyd Bookey, it all started with a great idea. As head of the kindergarten through twelfth-grade education outreach team for Google, she knew that many parents struggled to sort through all of the available books, apps, and other educational tools for their kids. When she became a mom herself (her children are now preschoolers), she felt the challenge even more personally. "I suddenly felt confused about which resources would work well for them," she recalls. "We were overwhelmed with the amount of information out there about educating our kids and wanted to find a way to help parents navigate this landscape for their individual child."

She decided to leave Google and launch Zoobean, which matches books, apps, and other resources with kids' preferences and interests. With a focus on families with children under the age of eight, she ends up doing a lot of testing in her own home, to make sure she's curating best matches for her small customers. Entrepreneur and investor Mark Cuban, one of the investors on ABC's *Shark Tank,* recognized the brilliance of the concept and invested $250,000 in the business after Bookey and her husband, Felix Lloyd, appeared on the show in 2014. Soon afterward, they raised an additional $400,000 and now continue to build their business, expanding into a partnership with libraries with a service called Beanstack. It allows libraries to license their system to offer personalized recommendations to local families.

While Bookey loves building a company that she knows is helping families, she also warns that the schedule can be even more grueling than a traditional job's. "The truth is, it's hard—much harder than my previous corporate job," she says. She's often working early in the morning before her children wake up and again in the evenings. Still, she likes that she's in control of those hours.

That's exactly what researchers who examined self-employed moms found. Nicholas Beutell, a management professor at Iona College, and Joy A. Schneer, a management professor at Rider University, found that while self-employed workers and workers at organizations report similar numbers of hours worked, those who are self-employed report higher levels of autonomy, flexibility, and life and family satisfaction.

Many moms have jobs that naturally lend themselves to flexible self-employment, which makes it easier to jump into the entrepreneurial life. According to the National Women's Business Council, there are around 7.8 million women-owned businesses in the country, and that number has been steadily growing.

Popular industries for women entrepreneurs include health care, education, retail, and recreation.

When I asked PayScale.com to send me the highest-paying jobs for "mompreneurs" who worked part-time, the list was topped with health care jobs. Family nurse practitioners, dental hygienists, and registered nurses all earn a median hourly wage of over $25, with family nurse practitioners at the top with a median hourly wage of just over $42.

The entrepreneurial moms that I interviewed offered these tips for other aspiring business owners:

- Create your own space. If you are launching a business from home, then you'll want to have your own dedicated space to working on it, even if it's a desk in the corner of the playroom. (That happens to be my own setup for my writing.) Setting some boundaries about where and when you're working can make it easier for the other members of your family to help you be productive.
- Protect your family finances. Depending on the size and type of your business, you might want to consider forming an LLC to help keep your personal assets and loans separate from your business-related ones. Liability insurance also offers protection, especially if you're at risk for getting sued. A cupcake catering business might sound innocent enough, but if you accidentally give a customer food poisoning, you don't want the incident to put your family's savings at risk. Consult with a lawyer or financial

professional to make sure you're getting the protection you need.

♦ Get ultraorganized with paperwork. When you have income and expenses coming in from a variety of sources as you build your business, you'll want to be sure to create a tracking system that keeps you from getting overwhelmed and makes it easy to file taxes, with or without the help of a tax accountant.

♦ Team up with other moms. When I was launching my new money planner shop on Etsy, I found a fellow mom on Etsy who created illustrated greeting cards. I hired her to make the covers for my planners and we have been working together ever since. Other moms are often interested in working with each other, for pay or skill trades. A mom blogger with marketing experience might write press releases for you in exchange for a few hours of your web design skills. Etsy, so-called mommy blogs, Facebook groups, and Meetup.com are all great places to connect.

♦ Keep start-up costs low. The boom of online e-commerce sites, including the ones mentioned here, makes it easier than ever to get a small business off the ground and running with very little in the way of start-up costs. You don't even need your own e-commerce website if you begin by selling your products or services on sites like Etsy or Fiverr or collect payments over PayPal. Keeping start-up costs low also gives you more flexibility to adjust your offerings based on what customers like and demand.

- Save and invest earnings. After paying off any out-standing high-interest-rate debts, smart moms save and invest the money their businesses bring in instead of spending more on lifestyle upgrades. That way, they can continue to grow their businesses without adding more pressure to earn. Even when earning outside of a traditional job with a 401(k), they find a way to contribute to their future retirement savings through Roth IRAs, traditional IRAs, or other types of savings accounts.

- Tap into your favorite skills. Moms excel when they're building businesses that tap into their deepest gifts and values, whether it's connecting with others, writing, or working with technology. If you're still brainstorming business ideas, reflect back on your favorite jobs in the past, hobbies, or even childhood pursuits. Browse e-commerce sites like Upwork (formerly oDesk and Elance) and Freelancer.com to see how other people are making money through products and services. Consider what your friends and family members ask for your help with, because anything from party planning skills or child-rearing expertise can turn into an income stream.

Entrepreneurial moms often report that their inspiration starts at home. Tamara Monosoff, author of *The Mom Inventors Handbook,* got her idea for a device that prevents kids from un-rolling toilet paper after watching how much her own children enjoyed unrolling an entire tube. Now she helps other moms come up with their own "million-dollar" ideas, from sandwich boxes to sippy cup straw cleaners. You never know when inspiration might strike, whether you're crouched over a bathtub or making your thousandth school lunch.

SMART MOM, RICH MOM
ACTION STEPS

1. Always be working and earning money in some capacity, even at a reduced level, to maintain your future earning power.

2. Look for nonlinear career paths, including entrepreneurship or freelance work, that might work for you and your career goals, especially during periods that you cut back hours in a traditional job.

3. If you have a full-time job, negotiate raises (and promotions or greater responsibility) regularly to make sure you are earning as much as you should be. Use websites like PayScale.com to check that you are being paid a competitive rate for your work.

4. Consider strategic pay cuts, especially if they allow you to continue working in a way that will let you stay in the workforce longer and in a more satisfying way. Manage and anticipate those fluctuations in earnings by creating an emergency fund that contains at least

six months' worth of expenses. Constantly reevaluate whether your career and family life are working together the way you want them to or whether it's time to make changes.

5. Flesh out a backup plan for yourself so that you have some ideas of what you would do if your current job disappeared. Do you have a side business in the works or a second career dream, like teaching, that you might want to pursue?

6. Maintain your personal brand online, so you are known for the skills that you want to bring to the marketplace. If you excel at web design, that should be highlighted in your LinkedIn and Twitter pages, along with recommendations from coworkers or clients. This strategy is especially important if you're taking breaks from the workforce, so you can more easily network and stay in touch with professionals in your field and opt back into work when you're ready.

7. If your income goes down temporarily, make sure you are still contributing to a short-term savings account as well as a retirement account. If you are not eligible for a 401(k), consider an IRA. In 2015 the Transamerica Center for Retirement Studies surveyed 1,600 self-described homemakers and found that just over half lack a plan for saving for retirement. You can set household income aside for retirement even when you're not working to prevent a gap in contributions. That way, your money for later years can continue to grow.

8. Take advantage of all available tax benefits to working parents; if you don't currently have access to traditional workplace benefits like life insurance, consider signing up for them privately. (For more details on life insurance and other protective measures, see Chapter 6, "Playing Defense.")

5

INVESTING MAMAS

A s the sun set over the golf course surrounding my grandmother's beachfront condo community in Florida, I huddled by the grills with my mom and grandmother. We sipped our gin and tonics while chatting with the woman next to us, who was struggling to get her grill hot enough to barbeque her hamburgers. "My husband always did this for me," she explained, looking a little embarrassed.

As the sky grew streaked with purple and pink and the mosquitoes came out to nip at our ankles, our conversation turned more serious. Her husband had died the previous year, leaving her to handle grilling—and a long list of other tasks—on her own. She had some words of advice for me before heading back inside with her dinner: "Women today should learn to do everything themselves. Don't wait until you have to."

It's a lesson that applies as easily to ground beef as it does to stocks. For the most part, we are going to be on our own at some point, whether through choice, tragedy, or the simple fact that wives tend to outlive their husbands. That's why we need to know how to manage our investments with the same confidence we apply to paying bills or planning the week's meals.

Traditionally, many of us have made the mistake of handing over those reins to our husbands. In a study on couples and retirement investments, Fidelity found that while the percentage of women taking ownership over long-term retirement decisions has grown, it's still just 19 percent. In fact, most women said they were more confident in the ability of their partners to manage retirement finances than their own.

Husbands tended to agree. They believe they are better at managing the investments and also are the ones to develop a personal relationship with the couples' financial adviser, if they had one. No wonder, then, that most women end up finding a new professional to work with after their husbands die.

Recognizing that women control a massive—and growing—amount of assets, the financial industry has been trying to address its "woman problem" by reaching out to us through webinars and pamphlets. One challenge is overcoming the gender imbalance of the industry itself. According to the Certified Financial Planner Board of Standards, only 23 percent of CFP professionals are women. (The board is working to change that by recruiting more young women into the field.)

We can't wait for the industry to change. But we can teach ourselves to embrace our inner investor now. That's what Angele McQuade did as a young mom who gave up her job as a radio production assistant so that she could care for her two children while her husband focused on earning his PhD. Lacking a financial role model, she decided to teach herself, so she started at the library, checking out books like *Investing for Dummies.*

When I met Angele on a rainy day at a local coffee shop, she lit up when she started explaining how she taught herself about investing. After reading as much as she could at the library, she began investing in the stock market and joined Better Investing, a nonprofit association. She learned how to invest in stocks and opened up retirement accounts for herself and her husband. "As we tried to reconcile our growing family's financial needs with my husband's small research stipend, I realized I might be able to stretch our limited income further by teaching myself more about personal finance," she says. That research led to her hosting investing workshops and teaching investing to her daughter's class, as well as writing for *BetterInvesting Magazine.* Later, she even authored two books on investment clubs and investing.

As her children grew older, she wanted to be able to tell them that they could attend any college they wanted. Her daughter, she explains, wants to be a theater stage manager, which means attending a four-year liberal arts college. "That kind of school comes with a big price tag," she says. Thanks to her savvy investments, Angele is prepared to help pay for it. "I so wanted our kids to have more financially than I did growing up. As a stay-at-home mom, learning more about money management and investing seemed like the most promising and profitable way I could help make that happen," she says.

McQuade fits the profile of a new kind of woman investor—the kind who relishes her role as the grower of family wealth. A 2014 Wells Fargo survey of over 1,800 women between age 40 and 80 with investable assets of $250,000 or more found that about half considered themselves to be the ones in charge of managing their family's investment accounts. (The younger women in the survey, those in their forties, were the most likely to say they were in charge.) Two in three women in the survey said they found it "exciting" to watch their investments in the stock market grow. Not surprisingly, most report being relatively prepared for their future retirements, with a median savings of $600,000 and goal of $1 million by the time they retire.

Smart moms embrace investing, because they know it's as essential an aspect of taking care of their families as wiping runny noses and reading bedtime stories. They usually start investing early, but if they're late bloomers, they make up for lost time by being more aggressive with their choices. They teach themselves as much as possible about their investing options by reading up on financial news and comparing the services offered by different financial providers to select the right fit for them. They prioritize managing their investments, devoting time regularly to reviewing their choices and making updates. If they decide to work with a financial professional, they choose one they feel a personal connection with, and keep close tabs on where their money is going and how it's being handled. Most important, they enjoy investing. It makes them feel good and confident about their own and their family's future.

___

FINDING YOUR INNER INVESTOR

Given the progress we've made toward gender equality since our grandmothers were coming of age, it is shocking how gendered investing culture still is. At a time when we tell our daughters that they can grow up to be anything they want, why is it that even young girls report talking less with their parents about money and investing than young boys? At an age where more women are earning graduate degrees than men, why is it that even in their twenties, men have already accumulated far higher investable assets than women? (The gap is $58,500 versus $31,400, according to the 2014 Wells Fargo Millennial Study.) And, perhaps most disturbingly, why are so many women so utterly unprepared for retirement when the time comes, leaving them dependent on other family members or in poverty?

According to the Transamerica Center for Retirement Studies, only 7 percent of women feel "very confident" in their ability to retire comfortably. No wonder, since a 2014 survey of over 4,000 workers by Transamerica found that women's retirement savings fell well behind men's in every age range. For women workers, median retirement savings were $47,000, compared to $74,000 for men. Women in their fifties, who are getting close to retirement age, had a median savings of just $70,000 in their retirement accounts.

Those figures help explain why the latest government statistics show that 12 percent of women over age 65 live in poverty; for divorced women, it's 21 percent. That's a lot of aging moms struggling to make ends meet.

In a system where retirements are primarily funded by our own savings and not company-sponsored pensions or a government paycheck, we have to learn how to invest, and wisely, if we want to enjoy those so-called golden years. Our lives quite literally depend on it. For younger women in their twenties and thirties, it's even more important. With more money flowing out of the system than into it, Social Security is constantly under fire. Benefits could be cut and retirement ages extended. For moms who spend time out of the workforce to take care of children or parents, Social Security benefits are already lower, because we don't get "credits" for those years. Payments are based on the highest thirty-five years of earning; if you've spent a chunk of your adult life out of the workforce, you might have "zeroes" entered for some of those years, which will reduce your monthly benefits. All of those factors put more pressure on our shoulders to fund our own futures without the safety net of government benefits.

In an event on retirement savings on Capitol Hill in 2014, Karen Wimbish, director of retail retirement at Wells Fargo, pointed out that young women are making the exact same mistakes when it comes to retirement savings as their mothers and grandmothers. They're afraid of the stock market and avoid risk, which means their money is not growing as fast as the investments of their male peers. The fact that women earn less on average also contributes to their lower than average savings rates and investable assets. The problem is compounded when those young women become moms and they start taking breaks from the workforce to focus on caregiving, further decreasing their income and, consequently, their savings.

A lack of financial confidence gets cited over and over again by studies trying to get to the bottom of women's investing handicap. Unfortunately, there's no way to inject ourselves with a secret potion of confidence in time to ratchet up our retirement accounts. Our feelings and attitudes often date back to childhood and the way we've watched our own parents (and especially our moms) manage their money, and those memories can't just be undone with a little pep talk from a financial adviser or financial workshop leader.

Like a bikini-clad baby boomer intent on participating in a polar bear swim on New Year's Eve, we have to just close our eyes and jump right in. It's going to be uncomfortable, perhaps even painful, but ultimately refreshing and even life changing.

Step number one is calculating your retirement number, or how much you need to have saved before you retire, so you know what your most important investment account—the one dedicated to your retirement account—is aiming for. You can go online and pull up an online retirement calculator (Bankrate.com or the financial institution holding your money are good places to start) that asks you a series of personal questions: When do you expect to retire? How much money do you make? How much do you put in your retirement account each month? The calculator will then spit out a number. The figure, which is likely to be well over $1 million and perhaps closer to $2 million or more, might just shock you into moving to the next step.

That next step is, not surprisingly, redirecting more money from your paycheck into your retirement accounts. If you have an employer that offers a 401(k), then you can do this automatically. You can sign up to have a percentage of your paycheck deducted and invested into your 401(k) each pay period. You can start with a modest percentage, like 5 percent, and gradually move up from there. On average, over your lifetime, you'll want to aim to put 15 percent of your paycheck into your retirement account. That's how much the Center for Retirement Research at Boston College estimates the typical household needs to put away. (Higher-income households need to save a higher percentage.) But the earlier you get started, the less you need to save, because the money has longer to grow.

In fact, the Center's analysis shows that if you start saving at age 25 and retire at age 67, you only need to put away 7 percent of your income into retirement accounts. But if you wait to age 35 to start, that percentage shoots up to 12 percent. If you don't start until age 45, you have to save 20 percent to achieve the same savings, which the Center defines as the ability to replace 70 percent of your income in retirement, a reasonable goal. (Depending on your income level, you might reach the annual pre-tax limit, which was $18,000 in 2015, for 401[k] contributions when saving these percentages, but you can still save an unlimited amount of after-tax earnings.)

In other words, while 10 percent is a good floor, 15 percent or 20 percent is a better target if you want to be able to comfortably replace your income in retirement. We can hope for a return to 10 percent average returns each year, as our grandparents experienced in the twentieth century, but counting on 6 percent returns is safer. That's one reason why Olivia Mitchell, an economist at the University of Pennsylvania's Wharton School and a thought leader in the field of retirement savings, urges her twentysomething daughters to save between 15 percent and 25 percent of their current income for retirement. (Another is their long life expectancy: She notes that one in four women born today will live to age 95.)

If you are self-employed, working part-time, or taking a break from the workforce altogether, then you might be eligible for a Roth IRA or traditional IRA. Roth IRAs are after-tax accounts; if your household income is less than the qualifying amount (for 2015, under $183,000 for married couples), then you can contribute up to the $5,500 limit (or an additional $1,000 if you are age 50 or over). The money is then generally not taxed when you take distributions in retirement. Traditional IRAs work much the same way, but the money is contributed pretax and then you pay taxes on the distributions later. Both options are particularly relevant to women who take breaks from the workforce to care for children, because even though they might not have the traditional workplace benefit of a 401(k), they can still contribute to IRAs, based on their partner's income, as long as they file a joint return. It's not the size of your income but how you save that will determine your future financial security. The limits might sound low, but if you invest $5,500 in an IRA today and it grows at a 7 percent rate, it will turn into $58,721 thirty-five years later. Do that a few times, and you'll be on your way to a significant nest egg.

Once you've set up your accounts, it's time to select your investments. Here's where it gets a little tricky and where a lot of people run into trouble. Women in particular have a tendency to be overly conservative when it comes to selecting investments for those retirement funds, which ends up hurting us in the long run. If we leave our money in safe spots, like money market funds, then it is safer, but it also won't grow at the rate we need it to over time to build significant wealth. Instead, we need to select funds that will grow over the long term, so our investments are working as hard as we are.

You might opt for an index fund, which mirrors a large swath of the market, or a target date fund, which automatically shifts money into more conservative investments as you get closer to retirement. You can also select an array of mutual funds available to you. The key principle to keep in mind is that risks and rewards go hand in hand, so if you choose a fund for its potentially high returns, it could also lose money. And as you get closer to retirement age, you'll want to shift into more conservative funds, so your assets aren't at risk of declining just as you need them. But if retirement is still decades away, then most of your money should be invested aggressively, in the stock market, through a broadly diversified index or target date fund. Whatever investments you choose, be sure to check in on them to make readjustments at least once a year.

If this selection process is confusing or overwhelming, you can and should seek extra help in the form of one-on-one consulting offered through your HR benefits or plan administrator or with a private fee-only financial adviser. Fee-only advisers have an obligation to look out for your best interests, and they aren't paid based on the products they sell to you. Communication style is also worth considering; if you prefer email and Skype to in-person meetings, make sure your adviser is available for that. You want to make sure you enjoy working with your adviser. Remember, advisers don't always know how to talk with women clients, and they sometimes end up sounding condescending or sexist, so be sure you know they're on your side, because that's what you are paying them for.

LOVE AND MONEY

Within a relationship, there's nothing wrong with a little specialization. That's arguably one of the greatest benefits of marriage. You might cook the meals while he takes out the trash; he might always fill up the car with gas while you make the beds. With money, though, specialization can end up being bad for everybody, because despite stereotypes, women are actually better investors in many ways than their male partners.

A Fidelity white paper on women and investing observes that women tend to be strong researchers and planners—both of which are assets when it comes to investing. While men have a tendency to be overly confident, women look for more information and guidance before making decisions. Women also are less likely to get spooked by market dips, leaving money in the market to ride out the downturns, which helps them in the long run. Unlike men, they don't try to "beat the market," which is impossible. A higher percentage of men also make the mistake of putting all of their money in stocks (11 percent of men versus 8.1 percent of women). In addition, Fidelity points out that women save a higher percentage of their income for retirement, even though they earn less. On average, women contribute 8.3 percent of their income into retirement accounts, compared to 7.9 percent for men.

Women's proclivity for investing was driven home to me even more by Meredith Jones, a financial professional who studies the performance of funds managed by women. Her 2015 book, *Women of the Street: Why Female Money Managers Generate*

Higher Returns (and How You Can Too), documents women's investing advantage: We tend to trade less, sticking with a chosen strategy and avoiding the volatility (and fees) that can come from more frequent trading. "Women tend to be very disciplined investors," she says. In addition to pushing for more diversity in the finance industry, Jones urges men in the finance industry to adapt some of these strategies that women money managers often follow.

Given all these smart choices we make on our own, why are so many of us still deferring to our husbands when it comes to our joint accounts? I must admit, early in my marriage, I fell into this trap myself. When we got married, we combined all of our savings accounts and I pretty much let my husband manage them. I knew, vaguely, how much money we had in our accounts and how to access them, but I didn't oversee them any more carefully than that. My husband kept a password-protected Excel spreadsheet of our finances, and I did not, I am embarrassed to say, even know the password. (I only recently asked for it as I wrote this chapter.)

It sounds as retro as a *Downton Abbey* episode; in fact, a season five dialogue exchange on that early twentieth-century TV drama felt a little too familiar: Mrs. Patmore, the cook, tells Mrs. Hughes, the housekeeper, that Mr. Carson, the butler, has suggested she invest her money in a local building firm, but she isn't sure that it's a smart move. Mrs. Patmore says she doesn't want to put her money into something she doesn't understand, a sentiment that Warren Buffett himself has expressed. When Mrs. Hughes asks her why she even bothered asking Mr. Carson's advice, Mrs. Patmore responds that the only reason is his gender.

Handing over financial control to the men in our lives is a problem for many reasons. In extreme cases, it can be an early sign of an abusive relationship. According to research by Judy Postmus, director of the Center on Violence Against Women and Children at Rutgers University's School of Social Work, abusers often control the couple's finances, withhold information, deny women access to funds, and even ruin their victims' credit history on purpose and interfere with their ability to earn money. In fact, a financial education program that she found to be useful in helping survivors rebuild their lives starts with a lesson on economic security: how to make sure you always have access to cash and build credit by having accounts in your own name and carefully storing important financial and personal records, like birth certificates or Social Security cards. Even if we opt for separate accounts, as many married couples do, we should still be aware of how our household money is being spent and know how to access those accounts. Financially controlling behaviors, Postmus says, are red flags that can indicate an unhealthy and even abusive relationship.

While most of us are thankfully not in abusive relationships, we are modeling financial behavior for our daughters (and sons) just by how we conduct our lives, and that is enough of a reason for me to take a more active and vocal role in managing our investments. As if that's not enough of a reason, there are also more practical reasons: You can make better investment decisions together than your partner can alone, as the Fidelity paper shows. You also want to have immediate access to funds in the event of tragedy, like your partner's unexpected death. When we met with our estate planning lawyer to draft our wills and he walked us through our various financial accounts, I realized that my name wasn't even on all of my husband's financial accounts, a situation we quickly fixed. Finally, the fact that we are likely to outlive our husbands means that at some point, we will be managing these accounts ourselves, and we don't want to be logging in for the first time, faced with investment decisions, in a grief-stricken and elderly state. I'd rather get my practice in, and make my mistakes, early.

If you are ready to embrace your financial duties within your marriage, here are some conversation starters to kick things off. You and your spouse can make it fun by setting aside a child-free hour, supplementing it with the beverage of your choice, and doing something enjoyable afterward, like going on a real date.

◆ Where is our money now? A list of accounts, along with any relevant account numbers, contact information, and related passwords, is useful and should be updated annually and stored in a secure location, either digitally on your computer or in a secure file at home.

◆ What is our investment strategy? What are our priorities? If you are building retirement savings accounts, then you'll want to review how much each person is currently contributing and how it's invested. If you are saving for a big purchase, like a house, then you'll want to be directing money into a conservative, short-term savings spot, like a money market fund.

◆ What financial action steps do we need to take in the next year? What about the next five years? Ideas include meeting with a financial planner, taking out more life insurance, or opening a 529 account for tuition.

◆ Is there anything about our financial life that we want to change? Spending less is a common goal.

◆ How prepared are we to handle an unexpected crisis, such as a job loss, long-term health problem, or a needy family member? Taking on caregiving duties for an aging parent or giving money to a relative in need are common events that can place a lot of financial and emotional strain on couples, which is compounded if you disagree on how to handle it.

This money talk can become a regular part of your relationship. These conversations might sound difficult, especially if you haven't been having them, but they actually tend to improve your love life, and maybe even your sex life. JoAnneh Nagler, a yoga teacher, money coach, and author of *The Debt-Free Spending Plan,* says that when she started talking about money and developing a spending plan to help pay off debt with her husband, they discovered that the money talk could be an aphrodisiac, largely because it reduced their stress levels. Paying off $80,000 in debt that had been following her for years made her feel freer and friskier. If that's not a good motivator, I don't know what is.

TO THE FUTURE AND BEYOND

For a lot of us, retirement is only one of the long-term goals that we are saving and investing for. The other is college. We want to be able to send our kids to college and watch them graduate without incurring a crippling amount of student loan debt. The *Washington Post*'s personal finance columnist, Michelle Single-tary, goes as far as to say that parents have a moral obligation to pay for college, since the degree is all but required for success in today's economy.

Whether you agree with that moral imperative or not, it sure would be nice to look into our kids' eyes and tell them they can go to any school that they want and that money is not a limiting factor. That's one of the reasons Angele McQuade felt so moti-vated to teach herself about investing. It's one of my top con-cerns, too. Unfortunately, it's often in direct conflict with our own financial security.

The saving for retirement versus saving for college choice is one that all parents face. A 2014 survey by Allianz found that among single parents, the pressure to choose between the two is especially high: Three in four respondents said that trying to do both is stressful, especially among single moms, who brought home an average of $78,800. Eight in ten single moms said they were stressed out about trying to save for college and retirement simultaneously.

If you only have room in your budget for one big savings goal, then it should be your retirement (and that's after the even more pressing matter of having an emergency fund of at least six months' worth of savings). There's simply no one else who is going to fund your nonworking years, and if you are living in poverty, it will be a massive burden to your children, assuming they are even in a place where they can help you. When it comes to college tuition, kids can always choose a less expensive school, or they can work to put themselves through college or take out loans.

If you have some flexibility to fund both goals, though, then you can open a 529 college savings account, which offers tax advantages, including no federal taxes on the earnings. Some states also offer deductions for money contributed into their own plans. (States sponsor their own plans; although you are free to choose any plan, you might benefit more, taxwise, from choosing your own state's plan.) An analysis done by Vanguard for the *New York Times* showed that if you put $5,000 a year into a 529 savings account that grows 6 percent a year, then after eighteen years you'll have $179,140 in the account for education expenses. (You can also play around with your own numbers using college savings calculators at FINRA.org, Bankrate.com, Fidelity.com, or your own financial institution.)

Some employers offer the option of direct deposit from your paycheck into a college savings account, which can make it easier to automate savings. You can also open a regular, after-tax savings account dedicated to future college costs. As with a retirement account, you can shift the money into more conservative investments as your child approaches the end of high school, or pick a target date fund that makes those shifts for you. The investing principles are the same: You want to select low-fee or no-fee investments that offer broad exposure to the market. If you're too conservative, the money won't grow fast enough to pay the tuition bills. (The website Savingforcollege.com is a great planning resource, and your own state's college savings plan may offer state-specific guidance.)

If you live in a state that offers prepaid tuition plans, another option is to lock in tuition at today's price for later, regardless of how much tuition goes up. You can apply the money to tuition at any school in the country, including private ones.

Weighing all of these different options, and juggling competing priorities, requires making some judgment calls and, ultimately, jumping in, even in the face of some uncertainty. For years after the birth of our daughter, my husband and I put off opening a 529 account. It seemed complicated, requiring paperwork and another account to monitor. For a while, we even convinced ourselves we didn't need one. We figured we'd just dig into our regular savings when the time came or somehow come up with the cash through a new income source (the lottery, perhaps?).

Researching for this chapter, though, showed me how wrong we were. I knew that the smartest moms I was interviewing had opened 529 accounts because they didn't want to miss out on those tax savings, and they were also planners. They weren't counting on some miraculous nest egg to drop down as soon as their sons and daughters were ready for school—and I shouldn't be, either.

So before watching TV one night, we had a mini–money talk and agreed it was time for us to investigate our 529 options and finally open up accounts, one for each of our children. Some simple math showed us that we could easily save thousands of dollars by opening up a 529 account where earnings would not be subject to federal taxes, compared to sticking with our original plan of relying on regular after-tax savings. I researched my options the next day using the U.S. News 529 Finder and quickly learned that, as residents of Maryland, we could enjoy the full tax benefits, including a state tax deduction for contributions, if we opened up a Maryland college savings account. (Every state has its own tax laws, so you'll want to check out the options in your state. Usually the state website is a good place to start. And the money can still go toward tuition in any state, not just your own.)

Once that decision was made and I tracked down each of our children's Social Security numbers, it took me about ten minutes to fill out the online forms and get the accounts set up. Now, we'll check in at least once a year, transfer more money into the account, and build those savings so that we are ready—at least financially—when it's time for our daughter and son to head off to school. I regret not starting a college savings account sooner, when our daughter was born five years ago, but I also know that forgiving yourself and moving on from past money mistakes is an essential trait of smart moms.

SMART MOM, RICH MOM
ACTION STEPS

1. Embrace investing as an important aspect of your life. If you do not yet have your own investment account, such as a retirement account in the form of a Roth IRA or 401(k) through an employer, then open one.

Read up on different types of securities with a special focus on index funds that track the market and target date funds that shift their level of risk over time, making your investments more conservative as you get older. If you are currently taking a break from the workforce to care for children, you can still save in an IRA (often called a spousal IRA), based on your partner's earnings, as long as you file a joint tax return. If you are already maxing out tax-advantaged retirement accounts, then you can save more money for retirement in a regular account. That can help compensate for lower Social Security payments because of time spent caregiving or future benefit cuts.

2. Review and rebalance the investment accounts that you have at least once a year. In general, it makes sense to shift into more conservative investments, like bonds or Treasuries, and out of the stock market as you get closer to needing the money—the year you plan to retire or, with college savings, the year your child will begin college. (Target date funds make these shifts for you.)

3. If you share investing accounts with your husband, make sure that you do not abdicate all management power to him. You should know how to access every account (which means having any passwords or contact information) and make investment decisions together. Plan regular dates every few months to go over all joint saving and investment accounts and tackle any action steps together. (And by the way, if

you're the one in charge of the finances, as many smart moms are, make sure your partner knows enough to take over if necessary or to fill in temporarily in your absence.)

4. Calculate the amount of money you should strive to save before retiring, based on your current salary, expected retirement date, and other factors, using an online retirement calculator offered through Bankrate.com or your own financial institution. Aim to average at least a 15 percent savings rate over your working years.

5. Sign up for the long-term investment and savings accounts that come with tax advantages that are available to you, including a 529 for college savings if it makes sense for your budget and a 401(k) or Roth IRA (or traditional IRA) for retirement. Aim to put at least 10 percent of your income into a retirement account like a 401(k) automatically, and a higher percentage if you got started after age 30. (If that sounds like a lot, start with a lower percentage and slowly work up to it.) Pick up any match offered through your employer.

6. Minimize the fees that you pay on your investment accounts by selecting investments that carry low management fees, like index funds; always ask first about the fees involved before working with a professional or moving your money into a new account.

7. If managing your long-term investments feels overwhelming and you are having trouble deciding how

to invest, then get help. Start with any available work-place programs through your own or your partner's employer. Many companies—and the financial ser-vices firms that manage retirement accounts for them—offer free workshops and one-on-one consult-ing for employees enrolled in retirement accounts. If that's not available, then consider working with a fee-only financial adviser who can guide you. You can find one at the website of the National Association of Personal Financial Advisors (NAPFA.org). And if you ever feel like your financial adviser is talking down to you or doesn't understand what kind of help you need, find a new one.

8. Prioritize saving for your retirement over saving for your children's future college tuition. They can always work and take out loans (along with choosing a cheaper school), but you have no other alternatives for funding your retirement other than building up a signif-icant nest egg.

6

PLAYING DEFENSE

When Barbara Stanny was growing up, her father, one of the founders of H&R Block, often told her not to worry about money. "My father was very old-school," she recalls. "He believed making and managing money was a man's job." The only thing she remembers him telling her about money was, "Don't worry."

Later, after she got married and became a mom to three daughters, she found herself unprepared when her husband started gambling away their money. "Over the course of our fifteen-year marriage, he lost a fortune of my inheritance, and I continued to let him manage the money because of how intimidated I was by it," she says. They eventually got divorced and Stanny was left with over $1 million in tax bills. She didn't have the money to pay the IRS and her father wouldn't bail her out.

That, Stanny says, was the rock-bottom point that forced her into a crash course in managing money. She started reading as much as she could about investing, taking classes and writing about money in her new career as a financial journalist. She eventually took care of her tax bills and rebuilt her own financial security, as her daughters watched. She learned how to grow her income over time, too. "I simply raised my fees. . . . I knew I deserved to earn more for no other reason than I'm worth it," she says. When she remarried, she made sure not to repeat her previous mistake: She kept her money separate and handled her own investments. Now a grandmother, she writes, talks, and coaches other women to manage their own cash to help them avoid her own costly errors.

Stanny's experience with a midlife money crisis is, unfortunately, a common one. In Alexandra Fuller's 2015 memoir *Leaving Before the Rains Come,* which tells the story of her marriage and subsequent painful separation from her husband, she says she was happy to turn over her finances to her husband after they got married. "Charlie had taken control of the money side of my business from the very start. When the checks arrived from my agents, they went straight to him. I didn't have a credit card in my own name; there was nothing under my own Social Security number," she writes.

That system worked fine until their relationship stumbled. Her husband's real estate business suffered in the Great Recession and the fact that she knew so little about her money turned into further fuel for their fights. Fuller recalls arguing as their marriage fell apart: "Me saying again that I didn't understand our investments; that I had trusted him not to get us here in the first place. Him saying that he had been trying to tell me all along things hadn't worked out so well for us; that I had been an active participant in our economic demise."

In her 2006 memoir, *Money, a Memoir,* Liz Perle shares a similar story: "He liked to control the cash, pay the bills, invest the money, and govern the expenses. That was more than fine with me," she writes of her first husband. When he suddenly wanted a divorce, she found herself unaware of even where their money was and how to access it, much less manage it.

Divorce is just one of many life experiences that can bring on a financial crisis in a mom's life. Death, accidents that leave a husband incapacitated, and illnesses are also among the twists and turns that life can show us. Even financial dishonesty, such as a partner who hides a debt problem, can wreak havoc on your family's finances. These are not fun outcomes to consider. Most of us, myself included, would prefer to ignore the potential for terrible things happening to ourselves and the people we love. But since we are the grown-ups here, and little people are relying on us, we have to force ourselves to take steps to protect our families. We don't have to dwell on it or be maudlin for long, but consider this: Women are far more likely than men to outlive their spouse by a factor of four to one. The U.S. Census Bureau reports that for those between the ages of 40 and 44, there are 170,000 widows in the country, compared with just 52,000 widowers, and the numbers only go up from there. According to the Bureau of Labor Statistics, about 42 percent of marriages end in divorce by age 46. And one in four young people will become disabled before retirement age, according to the Council for Disability Awareness.

If those numbers don't spur us into action, perhaps other women's life stories will. Memoirs, history books, and movies are filled with cautionary tales. I found myself struck again by the truth that all moms need to manage their own money while watching *The Widow Lincoln,* a play about Mary Todd Lincoln, the grieving widow of President Lincoln and mother of two young sons, after he was shot to death. In the midst of her emotional meltdown, she wonders how she is going to manage her finances, now that she has no income and no husband. "How will I ever pay these debts?" she asks, a question from 1865 that still resonates 150 years later.

Just as getting familiar with our future selves can help us save for retirement today, so too can opening our eyes to the experiences of women who experience the heartache of divorce, death, and other crises. If a woman in your family has firsthand experience with rebuilding her life after that kind of turn, then ask her to tell you her story. How did she do it? What made it easier or harder to move forward? The subject may still be raw and she may not want to talk about it, but she might, especially over tea or wine on a quiet afternoon or evening.

Those conversations can lead to honest ones with ourselves: Would we be able to manage our money solo if we suddenly had to? Could we still afford our mortgage and other basic costs if our partner's income suddenly disappeared? Do we have the estate planning documents and insurance policies in place that would help us transition into life as a single mom if we had to?

Smart moms are not in denial about the almost certainty that we will be managing our money on our own one day, for one reason or another. Most of the smart moms I interviewed manage their finances throughout all stages of their relationships so that when they have to do so on their own, it is not a shock. They know which folders and documents to turn to in case of a health emergency, they use financial tools like life insurance and disability insurance to guard against life's unexpected events, and they see their potential futures with open eyes. They protect their finances like mama bears defending their cubs because they know doing so means protecting the security of their families.

GETTING PAPERS IN ORDER

Feeling a sense of mastery over your finances and preparing to handle unexpected events starts with getting household paperwork in order. The task is quite challenging, especially when you have small children that seem to rack up as many government-issued documents in their first few years of life as you have accumulated over your own decades-long one.

When I first became a mom, I made the mistake of buying a new notebook to record every detail of my newborn daughter's visits to the doctor, along with a new filing system and a dozen colorful files, all of which I planned to use to store everything from pediatrician notes to her birth certificate to my own observations about her growth and development. I quickly realized that I was trying to store way too many things in one place, and her truly essential documents, like her newly minted Social Security card, were getting lost in a mix of health care documents.

By the time my son was born a few years later, I had a better system down pat. For each child, I keep one labeled file folder with their birth certificate and Social Security card. Separately, I keep a notebook on their development; it holds the letters I write to them when I am feeling particularly mushy and their pediatrician records from each well-visit during their first year. Nearby but also separate is my household file folder with tax receipts, home-related documents, estate planning details, and household maintenance records. That way, if I am out of town or otherwise unavailable when a pipe starts leaking, my husband would know whom to call—or at least where to look for the number.

Even though I try to keep the paperwork I save down to a minimum, I still face a buildup of unneeded medical receipts and other day-to-day living paraphernalia, so at least once a year I go through it all and make a pile of old papers to shred. That way, I can keep our household documents relatively organized and can locate the car's recall notice when we need it or pull up our gas utility's contact information when we have a problem.

These guidelines for setting up a household planning system can be adapted to fit your own circumstances:

- Select one location for the family's most valuable documents, including birth and marriage certificates, identification cards, records of assets (including homes and cars), and Social Security cards.
- Find a place to store household maintenance records along with contact information for repair services. Be sure to include records of household safety maintenance: smoke alarm testing and battery replacement, carbon monoxide alarms, radon testing, lead testing, and emergency kits. One copy of every regular household bill should also be stored here for the account contact information.
- Create a file for work-related benefits accounts,

including flex-spending accounts and the related receipts, so you can easily file them each year before the deadline.

◆ Make a written plan so that family members know what to do if there is a weather or other type of emergency that requires an unexpected evacuation or other disruption of a typical work and school day. Every home should also have emergency supplies that include first-aid kits, nonperishable food and water that could last for three days, working flashlights with extra batteries, and any medicine that family members need. Cash and contact numbers for other family members can also help, in case electricity is out for an extended period.

◆ Find a secure location for a list of financial accounts and other estate planning documents, including wills and health directives. At least one trusted person, such as a lawyer or family member, should have a copy or know how to find these documents. Getting these papers in order also gives couples the chance to talk through the various accounts and debts each person has, which will avoid unpleasant surprises or secrets later. Tools like FileThis offer secure digital storage for most kinds of financial documents, so you can cut down on paperwork and easily search for what you need. You can also use an app like JotNot to store documents that you want easy access to, like vaccine records or birth certificates. (If you suspect financial dishonesty or hidden money problems at home, then you'll want to take extra steps to protect yourself and your children. Valerie Rind's book, *Gold Diggers and Deadbeat Dads,* is a great place to start.)

◆ Create a file for the current year's tax receipts or have a method for storing them digitally (apps like Shoeboxed can help with online storage).

◆ Use a digital storage system that backs up family documents, photos, and videos. An external hard drive or cloud-based service is recommended so that you can recover these items even if your computer crashes.

◆ Make sure a partner or trusted person has at least a general knowledge of where to find these files, in case you are unavailable when they are needed. Even moms get the flu, break legs, or face a number of other life events that keep them out of the game long enough to have to let someone else temporarily take over.

Even the most organized systems need regular review at least once a year to pare back older papers and shred the ones that contain personal information but are no longer needed. If you are using a relatively small space, like a file box, to contain all your paperwork, then it forces you to sort through and get rid of the older documents on a regular basis. When I can't cram any more papers into my own filing box, I know it's time to schedule an hour to sort through it all. You can also store as much as possible online to further minimize the paperwork; just make sure it's stored behind a secure, password-protected firewall.

While most of us could get by using a jerry-rigged system of shoeboxes and piles of paper, a system that doesn't make sense to anyone but you could make it very difficult for someone, even a husband, to take over in our absence, whether we're on a work trip or in the hospital. And having a system that's practically worthy of a Container Store photo shoot makes running the household easier and more enjoyable for us in the meantime, too. It can also save you cash: It's much easier to negotiate with your cable company or ask for a refund on a misprocessed health insurance claim if you have the paper trail to help you make your case.

PROTECTING YOURSELF AND YOUR FAMILY

Talking about certain subjects, such as taking out life insurance, appointing guardians for children in the event of your death, and other types of estate planning, are about as uplifting and joyful as your annual appointment with your gynecologist, and even less relaxing. These discussions force you to think about your worst fears: death and leaving your children parentless.

But we've got to do it because, well, it's our job. No one else is going to make sure our kids are protected in our (unlikely) absence. The absolute necessities in our responsible parenting toolkit include having life insurance and a will (including the appointment of guardians for children). Health care directives that specify preferences for medical decisions and a power of attorney to designate who you want to help you manage your finances in case you are unable to do so are also valuable. While many of these forms are available online and some websites even offer state-by-state customization, the safest option is to work with a professional who can ensure that you are following all applicable laws so that you and your family are protected and your documents are considered valid and final. Working with a lawyer can cost anywhere from $1,000 to $3,000 or even more for complicated family situations, but it is generally a onetime expense that can save your family money, and trouble, in the long run.

First, life insurance: How much should you get, and how? If you or your partner have full-time jobs, then you likely have some life insurance through your employer, but chances are it's nowhere near the amount you would need to really replace your income if you (or your partner) were suddenly gone. If you don't know how much insurance you currently have as part of your benefits package, ask your human resources department. That way, you can figure out how much more to take out.

A general rule of thumb is to take out at least ten times your income, although you can calculate a more accurate estimate by adding up all of the expenses you would want to pay for in the event of your or your partner's death and subsequent loss of family income. College tuition, the mortgage, and day-to-day expenses for a couple decades are among the costs to include on that list. If one person earns less but handles many of the day-to-day household and parenting tasks, then consider the costs you would incur if that person were no longer around. The surviving spouse might need to hire additional help as well as scale back work hours to spend more time at home, which could also decrease household income.

You can take out supplemental insurance on the private insurance market, and the good news is that it's not that expensive, especially if you take out term life insurance when you are young and healthy. If you're a healthy thirty-five-year-old, for example, then you can likely buy a twenty-year term policy for $250,000 for under $250 a year. (The websites LifeHappens.org, SmartAsset.com, and Bankrate.com also offer helpful life insurance calculators.)

To get the best quote, you can use an online comparison tool or call around to a few companies to ask for estimates, just like taking out a mortgage. They'll ask you a few questions about your health, lifestyle, and family history. If you decide to proceed, a health professional will come to your home and take some blood and then soon after you'll hear that you have been approved. (The life insurance industry is trying to streamline this process, since it's a pain for busy people, especially parents. Soon, you might be able to take out policies under half a million dollars without the blood test.)

Life insurance isn't the only type of insurance to consider; a whole array of policies offer protection from various calamities that can strike, from as significant and life-altering as a disability to as (relatively) minor as a stolen diamond ring. Taking out renters insurance, homeowners insurance (along with any relevant riders for valuable items like artwork or jewelry), liability insurance if you run a small business, and umbrella insurance to protect you above and beyond your auto and homeowners policy can all help protect you and your family from adverse events.

Disability insurance in particular tends to get overlooked. The Hartford Financial Services Group reports that fewer than half of workers in their twenties and early thirties who are just starting out with young families have short-term disability insurance, and just 39 percent have long-term disability insurance. That's despite the fact that the average worker starting out has a three in ten chance of being disabled and unable to work before hitting retirement age. Just as with life insurance, you can supplement any disability insurance you receive through work with private insurance. You might even be eligible to do so through your employer for a better deal.

In many ways, protecting your own earning power by continuing to work and make your own money offers its own powerful form of insurance against a partner's death or disability. If you can support your family on your own if you need to, then you will be better able to keep your family on financially secure footing. Debra Muth, a holistic health practitioner who lives outside Milwaukee with her husband and their three children, found herself facing this challenge when her husband, Dennis, a maintenance mechanic, seriously injured his back at work one day in 2006. Ten years later, the pain continues and he's unable to return to work. While the family received some money as compensation for the injury, it is not nearly enough to replace Dennis's former income of around $52,000 a year.

If Debra hadn't continued building her own holistic health care practice, the family, including their young children, would have faced much greater financial hardship than they did. She documented the family's struggle in a book, *The Dark Side of Injury*, in which she urges other families to prepare for such a potential disability by taking out life insurance and advocating on behalf of your loved ones if they have to navigate the medical and insurance systems. "My salary has increased over time, but it's a huge challenge if it's the primary breadwinner [who gets injured]," she says.

Not that preparing for such circumstances is an easy thing to do. As my husband and I worked on our wills with a lawyer and took out supplemental life insurance, I felt a general malaise settle over me. I did not want to exchange emails about where my favorite necklace would go or what we would want to be able to pay for with life insurance proceeds or, even worse, what our funeral arrangements would be. It was downright depressing. But after we got it all sorted out, which took a few weeks, we were done thinking about it. We haven't had to revisit the topic since, except to update our documents after our son was born. It's a painful process, but a relatively quick one, and it gives you peace of mind to know your family will be protected, at least financially and legally, which are within your control.

As dismal as it is to face these topics head-on, much worse is to ignore them. According to a 2014 New York Life survey of 897 widows and widowers, widows said that they wished they had some or else more life insurance (47 percent), more savings (42 percent), more detailed financial discussions in advance (30 percent), a better financial plan (28 percent), and more organization of important paperwork (18 percent). Women who lost a spouse were far more likely than men to report they had to adjust to a reduced income and cut back their spending. They were also more likely to say they could no longer afford vacation and had not saved enough for retirement. On average, life insurance proceeds lasted almost two and a half years, but they wished the money could have lasted fourteen years. Wise words from women who have been there.

DIGITAL ASSETS

Digital assets, including social media accounts, also deserve some attention. If you are a frequent Facebook user, then your account is probably filled with years' worth of photos, comments, and snippets from your life—all of which would likely be valuable to your children after your death, especially as they get older. Would you want your account memorialized? Deleted? Or do you prefer to appoint a "legacy contact," as Facebook allows, to manage your account for you?

Any websites, blogs, or social media accounts (e.g., Pinterest, Twitter) that you've managed over your life similarly contain information and details about the kind of person you are, your values, and your interests. Thanks to the sophisticated nature of online search tools, much of that data and even photos will be available for many years to come, possibly even when your children and future grandchildren are surfing the Web. They might even learn more about who you were in life from what you have shared online. Your online presence is part of your legacy, and how others will learn about you in the future, perhaps even generations into the future, so you want to think about what story you are telling about yourself and your family online.

If the idea of people you don't yet know learning about who you are from your online presence makes you uncomfortable, then you can also sign up to have your Facebook account automatically deleted if you die, and in life, you can heighten your privacy settings so that the general public doesn't have access to your posts and photos.

You also want to make sure your privacy and security are protected—now and in the future, even after death. Make sure your birth date and mother's maiden name—which might be easy to figure out if you are friends with your own mom on Facebook—are hidden through your privacy controls, since those are common identity verification questions used on financial accounts.

Just as you maintain an updated overview of financial accounts and relevant passwords that you share with a trusted person, you should take a similar approach to all of your online accounts, including on social media. That way, your appointed person can manage or shut down the accounts in the way that you want. (Be sure not to include passwords and other sensitive information in your will, since that is a public document.) There are also a slew of new tools that can help you think through all of these issues, including Everplans.com, EstateMap.com, and RedFolder.com.

All of this planning helps not just in the case of tragedy, but also just in case of unexpected events: If you are traveling and your Twitter account gets hacked into, it's easier for your partner to help you if he knows how to access it on your behalf.

CULTIVATING FINANCIAL RESILIENCE

In my job as a personal finance columnist, I often receive heartbreaking letters from readers who want my help sorting out their challenging financial lives. Many of these letters are from moms, whose stress is compounded by the fear they have that they are letting their children down.

"I really don't know what to do with my debt," began one letter writer, who explained that although she has a college degree in health education, she has not been able to find work in her field. "I'm homeless and want to go to nursing school. I have student loans to pay, I need a place to live, and I have to support my children. What can I do financially to put my life together?" she asked.

Another wrote,

> I am a thirty-year-old mother of two. I am on a limited income and only make about $15,000 a year. My oldest daughter is nine years old and has special needs and my youngest is five. I would like to start saving for their future even if it's $10 to $20 a pay period. My biggest problem is that I can't keep a savings account open long enough without withdrawing funds.

As these women know, there is no magic solution that will solve their struggles. All they can do is make slow and steady progress out of the troubles they find themselves in. In both cases, raising their household income is a priority, which means finding higher-paying jobs that utilize their educational backgrounds. Opening up 529 accounts and making even modest contributions (after emergency savings accounts are funded) can reduce the temptation to use the money for current costs instead of saving it for future educational purposes. The reader with the daughter with special needs can also open a newly created 529A account to pay for future expenses like health care and transportation.

Both women would also benefit from making sure they own bank accounts in their own names, along with credit or debit cards, regardless of their relationship status, so they are building credit and have access to cash. Finding ways to stash away small amounts, as one of the women suggests, is one key to building up a sense of security. Saving loose change, cutting even nominal expenses, and skimming off money from each paycheck are all ways to slowly build up depleted savings accounts.

Knowing how to climb back out of a financial dark spot is one of the many crucial skills of motherhood. We have to be resilient for our children. Christine Hassler, a life coach and expert on bouncing back from disappointments, says these kinds of harrowing experiences can ultimately make us, and our families, stronger. She urges moms to take care of themselves first, which might mean investing in a new training program to strengthen their job-hunting abilities. "The best investment you can make is in yourself," she says. Hassler faced her own challenge when she got divorced just as the recession was also hitting her coaching and speaking business. "My husband was my financial security," she says. She kept building her business and ultimately found even more success, despite the economy.

Rebecca Dallek, a Washington, D.C.–based career coach who specializes in helping women navigate their careers, suggests taking small steps toward the new life that you want to create. If you want to change fields or get a new job, then speak to someone who has made a similar transition or attend a networking event. If even that is overwhelming, Dallek suggests a "pretend" exercise that anyone who has spent time with preschoolers will quickly grasp: If you are considering a big decision, such as a job change or move, then spend time pretending that you have already made that decision, and act accordingly. Apply for jobs, volunteer, seek out new connections "as if" you are pursuing that new life, Dallek suggests. When the trial period is over, you can see how it felt and decide whether you want to commit to that choice. It's a safe way to explore a big decision, Dallek says.

There's also comfort in the fact that hard times don't usually last forever. If you are climbing out of bankruptcy or have a poor credit history, then it can take up to seven years to rebuild and clear your name in the eyes of lenders, but it can take considerably less time to clear your own head and develop a plan for rebuilding.

Alexandra Fuller, the author who shared her divorce story in *Leaving Before the Rains Come,* started attending financial literacy classes with a group of other women who similarly had to start managing their own money. "Together we learned to read the numbers that had for so long frightened and confused us," she writes. She opened a bank account and a credit card in her own name. And she rebuilt her life, while raising her three children.

Elaine Williams, a widow and mom of three boys whom I first interviewed in 2008 for an article, took on extra data-entry work to compensate for the loss of her husband's income after he died of cancer. She soon built up a career as an author while also running a landscaping business as she raised her teenage and twenty-something sons. "Suddenly, everything is on you," she told me.

What smart moms know is that it actually always was on their shoulders, even if they didn't realize it until an unexpected event made it painfully clear.

SMART MOM, RICH MOM
ACTION STEPS

1. Organize existing paperwork related to your income and your household—financial accounts, estate planning documents like wills, tax-related receipts, health insurance documents, and mortgage information—in a clearly labeled binder that contains only up-to-date account information. Include relevant contact information so that if someone else had to suddenly take over management of the accounts, they could. Shred older paperwork that's no longer needed. If you store account information online, be sure that a trusted person, like your spouse or another family member, also has a copy of the information stored in a secure place.

2. Put your essential documents—including birth certificates and Social Security cards for every family member, marriage certificates, documentation of assets like your home and car, and copies of passports and driver's licenses—in a safe file folder or storage box that is in a secure, private location you can easily find quickly when needed.

3. Review your current insurance policies, including for health insurance, life insurance, dental insurance, homeowners or rental insurance, car insurance, and umbrella or liability insurance. Do you need to increase your coverage in any areas? Insurance calculators at LifeHappens.org, SmartAsset.com, and Bankrate.com

can help you figure out whether it's time to consider updating your policies with more coverage.

4. Take steps to protect your digital afterlife. Do your current social media accounts, including Twitter, Facebook, and any blogs or websites that you control, reflect the legacy you want to leave? Do they reveal any personal information, like your birth date, that would make it easier for a scam artist to break into your financial accounts? Make sure your online identity is protected in life and death. You can also refer to the "Legacy Checklist" in the handbook at the back of this book for an overview of estate planning preparation.

5. If you can, sit down and talk with an older woman in your family or a friend who has experienced loss in the form of divorce, death, or a partner who was unable to work because of a disability or illness. Ask them how they managed and learn what you can from their experience. Ask yourself if you would be prepared to handle your finances solo if you had to. If you're not ready, take steps to become more prepared. Review your finances with your partner, work with a financial professional, or take a class or workshop on money management.

You can also read memoirs by women who have survived these experiences to help with this thought experiment: Alexandra Fuller's *Leaving Before the Rains Come*, Barbara Stanny's *Sacred Success*, and Liz Perle's *Money, a Memoir* are just a few of my recommendations. Susan Gregory Thomas's *In Spite of*

Everything and Stacy Morrison's *Falling Apart in One Piece* are also powerful and thought-provoking. While she faces different financial issues than most moms, Sheryl Sandberg's poignant Facebook posts after her husband's unexpected death bring home the reality of grief and moving forward.

If you are already faced with the challenge of losing a partner, Alexandra Armstrong and Mary Donahue's *On Your Own: A Widow's Passage to Emotional and Financial Well-Being*, is a great resource, as is Jan Cullinane's *The Single Woman's Guide to Retirement*.

6. Cultivate your own financial resilience by making sure you protect your credit history, always have access and knowledge about the whereabouts of your savings and investments, and retain control over your investment and saving strategies.

7

STUCK IN THE MIDDLE

When Karen Cordaway was twenty-nine and pregnant with her second daughter, her mom got sick—really sick. She was terminally ill with carcinoma meningitis. Karen, who was working part-time as a substitute teacher and tutor at the time, scaled back her work schedule drastically and called on friends to care for her two-year-old so that she could be by her mom's side. She handled all the logistics of her mom's care, including decisions about treatments. "It was just a matter of time," she recalls.

Her mom died and then four months later, Karen's second daughter was born. She opted to continue scaling back her work schedule so she could be home with her two young daughters, sacrificing income to be the family's chief caregiver. "My income disappeared, but because I was always really frugal, we got by," says Karen, who lives in Connecticut. She saved by scaling back on haircuts, new clothes, and grocery purchases. Her husband, also a teacher, took on extra work teaching at night.

Even though Karen had always planned to return to working full-time, she still hasn't over ten years later, opting for part-time work instead. After her second daughter was born, she just never felt ready. "It was a combination of grieving and having the baby," she says. She did try a few different part-time jobs, including working as a sales rep, babysitting, and substitute teaching, but she resisted anything that required a set schedule because she always wanted to make sure she could be home for her daughters.

Now in her early forties, Karen continues to teach part-time while also writing and blogging about saving money, a topic inspired by her experiences. (I met her when she became a guest blogger on frugal shopping for *U.S. News & World Report.*) Her income might not be as high as when she worked full-time as a teacher, but for her, the flexibility that her part-time schedule allows is worth the financial sacrifice.

Karen's story is a familiar one for many moms. Moms are often the default caregivers in families—for children, for aging parents, and for other family members in need. We are often happy to embrace this caregiving role; it's a large part of our identities and a source of our deepest feelings of fulfillment.

As much as we embrace the role, though, we still often pay a financial price for it, as Karen has. The Family Wealth Advisors Council, a network of fee-only wealth management firms, found that women in their forties and fifties typically spent at least twenty hours a week on caregiving, either taking care of children or older family members, while also working paid jobs. The MetLife Study of Caregiving Costs to Working Caregivers put a price on all that love: On average, women give up $324,044 in lost earnings and retirement income, including Social Security benefits.

To lessen that financial toll, we can embrace our caregiving role while also planning for it. We can save money in advance to get us through lean times in case we have to scale back paid work. That strategy makes it easier to avoid taking on debt. We can have honest conversations with family members, including parents, siblings, and spouses, about who will be able to take on what responsibilities if and when an aging parent needs help. When it's not possible to work a full-time job, we can look for ways to embrace flexible and part-time earning opportunities so that we can continue to bring in some income while taking care of our loved ones.

After caring for our children, taking care of our aging parents is one of our biggest challenges as moms—financially, emotionally, and otherwise. Parents often need help when our children still need us, too, and as a result, it can often feel like we're trying to be there for everyone at once. It's easy to overlook taking care of ourselves. But taking care of ourselves, by protecting our savings and earning potential as well as our health and sanity, is the only way we can continue being there for everybody else. If we run out of money, or energy, then our families suffer, too.

CARING FOR THE CAREGIVER (YOU)

As a country, we are aging, and at some point, we are all going to need a little extra help. An increasing number of older adults can't take care of themselves and are turning to family members for help. According to Census Bureau data analyzed by the UCLA Center for Health Policy Research, the number of people over age 65 in the country will double over the next three decades. By the year 2030, the first of the baby boomers will start to turn 85 and require even more care. In fact, based on those demographic shifts, the AARP Public Policy Institute estimates that while there are currently seven family caregivers for every "vulnerable person," soon there will be just three. That means more pressure on the caregivers—and stress on moms.

Kenneth Matos, senior director of research at the Families and Work Institute, points out that in some ways, taking care of parents is even harder than taking care of kids. It tends to be less predictable and can require more extensive absences. If a parent in another city suddenly has a stroke, a son or daughter might need to drop everything to be by the parent's side for days or even weeks. When an otherwise healthy child gets ill, a parent might have to miss a few days of work, but usually not much more (at least until the next round of pinkeye hits).

At its root, caring for aging parents can be painful and sad whereas raising children is joyful and happy. Aging parents are dying; children are growing. The elder care experts I interviewed emphasized this difference over and over again. Our public debate on work-life balance centers almost entirely around parenthood, but a significant and growing number of us are also facing, or soon will be facing, caregiving for our aging parents. (And a portion of us will be handling both care for children and parents at the same time: A survey of staff members at the University of Rhode Island found that 12 percent pull double duty at home.) Those responsibilities could throw our lives, including our finances, completely out of whack.

Preparing for that caregiving role can help ease some of that stress. In addition to decreases in income from a scaled-back work schedule, caregiving can also be expensive, another reason for setting aside extra savings. A 2014 survey of 1,345 family caregivers by Caring.com found that almost half said they spend more than $5,000 a year on caregiving-related costs, including health care expenses. Half of respondents also said they had to change their own work schedules to accommodate their caregiving duties.

Sometimes, forward-thinking workplaces offer accommodations to caregivers that make it easier to juggle the dual roles of worker and caregiver. As we learned in Chapter 4, when the accounting firm PricewaterhouseCoopers changed its official firmwide policy so family caregivers could take unlimited sick days if their children or older family members needed them, they found employees were actually more productive. Other common policies in the workplace include flexible leave plans, information on elder care, dependent care assistance programs, and more control over schedules so that workers can leave early or late or work from home.

Family caregivers often end up paying more out of their own bank accounts than they have to because they misunderstand the laws and benefits available to their loved ones. Classic mistakes include not having key financial documents, like power of attorney, in place; paying for health care costs yourself instead of out of the loved one's bank accounts first, which can have a negative impact on Medicaid eligibility as well as tax and estate planning implications; and selecting paid caregivers that aren't covered by insurance policies. Veterans (and their spouses) and those under the federal poverty limit are also eligible for certain benefits; the website BenefitsCheckUp.org can help you figure out any benefits that might apply. (Families with complicated situations or significant assets might also want to enlist the support of an elder law attorney who can help with long-term planning and expense management.)

Indeed, managing your parents' money leads to a whole host of potential complications and pitfalls. If you put your own name on your parents' bank account, it can have the unintended consequence of triggering the gift tax and giving you all of their assets if they pass away, even if that was not the plan. (Your siblings might object, too.) It can also make you liable for their debts and them liable for yours. The helpful (and free) guides on "Managing Someone Else's Money," available through the website of the Consumer Financial Protection Bureau (cfpb.gov), can help you avoid those common mistakes. If you are the one in charge of your parents' money, then you have to make sure you are making decisions in their best interest and keeping their money completely separate from your own—hefty responsibilities, especially if you're also preparing their meals and bathing them each day.

Amid all their other duties, caregivers have to take care of themselves, too. Tapping into communities of other caregiving adults (Caring.com is one example) can help provide a sense of support. Caregivers can also outsource certain tasks, like cooking or errands, to help make their lives a little easier. If you are the family member responsible for day-to-day caregiving tasks, then perhaps siblings and other relatives can help cover the cost of some of this outside help, especially if they are not paying you for your caregiving work.

The most important self-care choice, perhaps, is to continue working, even if in a reduced way. Nell Lake, author of *The Caregivers: A Support Group's Stories of Slow Loss, Courage, and Love*, says that one in ten caregivers leave their jobs in order to take care of an older family member. That ends up having a lasting negative impact on their finances, not just in lost wages but in lost Social Security income as well, as the MetLife numbers show.

From a financial perspective, preparing to care for aging parents shares some similarities with preparing to have a baby—although it's easier to forget to prepare for the inevitability of parents who need help, perhaps. After all, there's no concrete nine-month time frame, burgeoning belly, or baby kicks to remind you to save more money to cover income breaks or to check on your work's leave policy and telecommuting options. Still, it's potentially as big—and life-changing—a caregiving role as parenthood. Talking through your family's plans, as uncomfortable as it can be, is one of the most powerful ways to get ready.

AWKWARD CONVERSATIONS

When Karen Cordaway's mom first got sick, she and Karen started talking more openly about how she wanted her affairs handled. At first, Karen didn't want to talk about death and dying with her, but soon she became more comfortable. "My mom and I were really close. She was really open about it and said, 'If something happens to me, I want to be cremated.' It's kind of weird that those topics come up, but once it gets really serious, a person does reveal some things," she says.

Those conversations helped Karen as she had to start making difficult decisions about radiation treatment versus painkillers and other end-of-life treatments. Many families, though, never have those difficult talks, largely because they can be so painful. The 2014 Fidelity Intra-Family Generational Finance Study of 1,058 parents and their adult children found that four in ten parents haven't shared the details of their retirement plans, including how they plan to cover living expenses, with their children. Around 15 percent have had no conversation about it whatsoever.

That lack of communication often leads to serious misunderstandings: Adult children, the Fidelity survey found, are likely to falsely believe their parents will call on them to provide financial help; almost all parents said they would need no such help. Adult children also tend to underestimate their parents' wealth by an average of $300,000.

When it comes to talking money with your parents, here are some strategies that can help you help your parents age gracefully. (For more ideas, you can flip to the "What to Ask Your Parents" list in the handbook at the end of the book.)

- ◆ Acknowledge that your parents have final say over their future, not you. It can be easy for adult children to want to take control or overstep their bounds; aging parents can be extremely sensitive to that. Resisting the urge to push your parents into a decision that you think is best for them can help preserve your relationship and their dignity. On the same note, respect their privacy; they don't need to share all of their financial details with you if they prefer not to.

♦ Make sure your parents have their documents in place and that you, or another trusted person, know where to find them. Those documents include health care directives, power of attorney documents, estate plans, life insurance policies, and wills. A family member should also know where to find an overview of financial accounts and how or where to access them, along with any relevant contact information or passwords.

♦ Keep talking. Situations and wishes are in constant flux, so this conversation is ideally one that happens regularly.

♦ Invite siblings into the conversation, too. Do you know how you would share caregiving duties if your parent suddenly needed daily or weekly care? Talking through scenarios ahead of time can ease the stress of emergencies.

♦ Be open to different types of living arrangements. If your parents become unable to live on their own, do you know if they prefer to live with you or in an assisted living environment? Adult children are often way off the mark when it comes to guessing their parents' preferences. The Fidelity survey found that just 6 percent of parents expected their children to directly care for them, compared to 43 percent of adult children who said they expected to do so.

One particularly awkward area to tackle with parents is money. Older adults may find managing their finances to be a challenge. Research suggests that adults in their sixties and seventies start struggling with basic responsibilities, including paying bills, calculating tips, or protecting themselves from telephone fraud. An adult child might notice bills piling up or a spike in charges on a credit card. Red flags identified by the National Endowment for Financial Education include slowness in completing basic financial tasks like filing taxes or paying bills, difficulty understanding bank statements, and difficulty calculating medical deductibles and understanding investment risk.

Since older adults also often have significant amounts of wealth to manage and protect after a lifetime of earning and saving, they could often benefit from some assistance from their concerned children. The AARP estimates that Americans over age 50 own about two-thirds of all bank deposits in the country. Without adding their name to bank accounts as co-owners (for the reasons previously mentioned), adult children can be added as contacts to bank accounts, to be alerted about potential fraud or unusual account activity. Adding access through a power of attorney document can also make it easier for you to help manage your family members' money if they are unexpectedly in the hospital or otherwise unable to manage it themselves.

Financial abuse, sadly a relatively common problem among the elderly, affecting as many as one in ten older adults, can also be identified and prevented this way. Some banks offer debit cards, like Visa's True Link, that only work at preapproved locations or that can be blocked at specific stores or charities that have caused trouble in the past. Asking questions and even just offering to organize paperwork can help protect your parents' money. According to a survey of 1,000 adults by Caring.com, few of us actually take these steps: 52 percent of adult children don't know where their parents store their documents related to estate planning and 58 percent don't know what's in those documents.

One couple I interviewed, Terrie and Jon Hull, discovered firsthand how aging can make parents financially vulnerable. After a car accident, Terrie's mom decided to marry her boyfriend, who later, along with her mom, accused Terrie of stealing her money. Not only did Terrie have to defend herself in court, but she had to fight to make sure her mom's money was protected, too. Terrie and Jon wrote a book, *A Legacy Undone,* about their experience and lead workshops to help families avoid the same fate. Their primary message is that families have to talk about how their money and estate will be managed well before anyone needs help, and they need to put those plans in writing. The conversations are only awkward, Jon emphasized, when families wait too long to have them.

As I was interviewing Terrie and Jon, it dawned on me that I had no idea how my parents organized their finances. Who is their lawyer? What are their health care preferences, if they become incapacitated? How would I even begin to sort through their financial accounts if I needed to? How would I access my dad's journal, which he's kept since I was a young girl and which contains priceless family memories? I've written countless articles on how important these conversations are, but I hadn't yet had one with my own parents. Still energetic in their sixties, they seem so young to me—far too young to ever need my help. After all, they are the ones giving me help with my kids most days. But realistically, over the next thirty years, chances are that the balance will shift at some point.

After getting off the phone with Terrie and Jon, I sent my parents an email. "Cognitive decline is just around the corner!" I wrote. "We need to discuss this while we are all still lucid!" They responded quickly with a few details and we planned on having a more in-depth discussion soon. I also made a mental note to review my own estate planning documents at home.

In fact, helping aging parents navigate their daily lives often has the welcome side effect of inspiring moms to make some changes to their own planning, too. Karen, who has two daughters, opted to make her will more specific, especially when it comes to who gets what. "I definitely don't want them fighting over anything," she says. Sometimes, caring for an aging parent gives you insight into your own potential future journey—and it might just scare us into making a few changes today or having that long-put-off conversation with a loved one.

SMART MOM, RICH MOM
ACTION STEPS

1. Start conversations with your parents about their plans, wishes, and preparations for the aging process. Also talk with your partner about the types of responsibilities you might be taking on, and how you can jointly prepare for them. Talk with other family members, including siblings, about how you can share duties.

2. Consider how you might be able to adapt a more flexible work schedule if you had to, including what types of income sacrifices you would have to make and how you can prepare for them. Check in on any available workplace perks, including dependent care assistance programs, sick leave policies, and tele-commuting options. Try to keep working in some ca-pacity, even a reduced one, if at all possible.

3. In addition to saving for retirement, college tuition, and other future goals, try to augment your short-term savings so that you could handle any antici-pated increased costs or drop in income that might come from additional caregiving responsibilities.

4. Do what you can to minimize the impact your care-giving responsibilities have on your own financial se-curity. Try to avoid paying for the expenses of relatives out of your bank account before their own funds are depleted; doing so can make it harder for them to qualify for Medicaid and also complicate their estate planning. Also be sure they are taking advantage of all the government programs available to them, especially if they are veterans or living under the federal poverty level.

5. Even when you are engaged in caregiving, remember to take care of yourself, too. That might mean asking for help from relatives or paying for services. Allevi-ating your own stress allows you to continue taking care of others.

6. When helping older relatives to manage their money, look for a bank that has experience with older patrons. Available services might include allowing you to add your name to monitor withdrawals without making you a co-owner of the account, or offering a debit card designed to prevent elder fraud. Simple accommodations, like offering access to a well-lit office without a glass partition for easy communication, especially for those who are hard of hearing, can also help.

8

MODEL MOMS

Susan Beacham, the CEO of Money Savvy Generation, a financial education company, and a passionate advocate for financial literacy, started teaching her daughters about money as soon as they began asking for things. As parents know, that starts at toddlerhood and never really ends. "You go into Target and see the dollar aisle and see things you didn't know you wanted, and then the child is disengaged [with the new toy] by the time you get home," she says.

So instead of buying those cheap toys in the checkout aisle, Beacham says she learned to say "No." That's how she imparted money lessons, including the one about delayed gratification, to her daughters, who are now in their twenties. (As an extra benefit, she adds, saying "no" so firmly also taught her daughters how to say "no," a valuable skill at all ages.)

Instead of buying them the latest Barbie or My Little Pony figurine on a whim, she showed her daughters how to stop and reflect on what might really bring lasting enjoyment and to save for it. After picking a future purchase, they tracked their savings progress with stickers. As soon as they were old enough (around ages eight or nine), she let her daughters make their own spending choices. "Instead of just saying, 'No,' you can say, 'You have the money in your spend account. Do you want to take it to the store?' It's very empowering to kids," Beacham explains. If they end up blowing their hard-earned cash on a toy that loses their interest quickly or breaks, then they've learned a useful lesson—another theme that emerged in my conversations with moms. "Money mistakes are very educational," Beacham says.

Her daughters also watch their mom doing the same thing with her money. "Whenever I'm doing something financial," she says, "whether it's giving a gift card or opening a bank account, I think, 'What message can I give my children?'" When they were younger and with her at the grocery store, Beacham would point out how she compared prices. At the pediatrician's office when she filled out forms, she made a point of showing her daughter that she was leaving the Social Security line blank, because the doctor's office didn't need it and sharing it would pose a security risk.

By starting all of those conversations early, it was easier to talk about real adult money problems when her daughters went to college and began their adult lives. "If your first talk about money is when they get their first job or open their 401(k), the conversation will be too awkward if you haven't started that conversation when they're younger," Beacham says. Now that her girls are young adults, the conversations have transitioned into more detailed discussions about grown-up budgeting and retailer loyalty programs. Same lessons, different details.

Around the same time as my conversation with Susan, a study came out from T. Rowe Price that left me disturbed and wondering if I was doing enough at home to teach my five-year-old daughter about money. The 2014 survey, which included 1,000 parents and 924 kids between the ages of eight and fourteen, found that while 58 percent of boys say their parents talked to them about setting financial goals, just 50 percent of girls say the same. Boys also believe they are smarter about money than girls do: 45 percent of boys consider themselves "very or extremely smart about money" versus 38 percent of girls. Parents said they think their sons are more likely to understand the value of a dollar compared to their daughters (80 percent versus 69 percent). Boys were twice as likely to have access to credit cards and more likely to say their parents are saving for their future college tuition (53 percent of boys versus 42 percent of girls).

Other studies have made similar findings. A 2011 Charles Schwab survey of teens found that boys are more likely than girls to say their parents talk to them about investing (23 percent versus 13 percent). Boys report knowing more about an array of financial topics, from protecting their personal information online to how credit card interest and fees work to what a 401(k) is.

Judith Ward, a senior financial planner at T. Rowe Price and mother of a son and daughter herself, made it clear to me that the responsibility for addressing this gender difference rests squarely on parents' shoulders. Boys, she explained, might just be more vocal about asking money questions, and as a result, they have more conversations with their parents about finances. "It comes down to parents being more proactive and making sure they're talking to their sons and daughters about these kinds of issues," she says. While parents don't intend to talk to their sons more about money than their daughters, it happens—unless we make a conscious effort to counter the tendency.

Like Beacham, Ward recommends using everyday experiences, like a trip to the grocery store or browsing clothing options on Amazon, as a chance to talk to kids about money. She often asks her kids to calculate the tip at restaurants for her or estimate discounts at a clothing store.

One of the clearest messages from the T. Rowe Price study is the connection between talking about money and feeling smart about it. When parents talk about college savings with their kids, their kids are more likely to say that they are saving for college on their own, too. Kids whose parents discuss the family finances with them are more likely to feel "smart" about money, and kids whose parents talk to them about setting financial goals are also more likely to consider themselves "savers." As with most tough parenting topics, talking is our first line of defense.

Money attitudes are passed on from parent to child almost as clearly as curly hair or full lips. We absorb phrases, habits, and attitudes that we see in our parents. I know I enjoy saving money today because my parents taught me the principles as a preteen, when they offered to match the savings I put away for college out of my allowance and summer job earnings. My mom helped me open my first retirement account as a twenty-two-year-old, and she didn't interfere when I sold my investments after a major loss when the tech bubble burst—my first tough lesson in investing. I haven't sold in a down market since.

Gender biases can get passed along, too. In addition to talking to our daughters about money, it also pays to consider the financial behavior you are modeling, or even how to counter the sexist messages they get from our culture. When Lego makes toys for girls that feature hair salons and shopping malls and when even "computer engineer Barbie" gets boys to handle the coding for her, parents have to offer a different reality. That starts with considering our own ingrained biases. One father I interviewed—an entrepreneur and financial expert—explained that he and his wife treat their sons and daughter equally, before adding that he expects that will become harder as his daughter gets older and wants more expensive things, "as girls do." He said this even after mentioning that his son had just splurged on a high-end, high-tech science toy. If even our dads expect us to spend more on clothes and shoes, then we just might fulfill that expectation.

Almost every mom I interviewed could point to a parent, grandparent, or other relative growing up who taught her to enjoy managing money—to not be afraid of it and to embrace personal finance as a key facet of growing up, as much as learning about birth control or how to clean a toilet. Those lessons didn't always stick right away, and they often had to recover from money mistakes they made as young women, but they could often recall that early inspiration decades later. We are role models for our daughters and sons, the next generation of parents. Our children are watching how we spend, save, invest, and give money. We can seek out opportunities to talk about money with our children, even if it's awkward at times or uncomfortable. We have a limited amount of time when we can impart specific lessons about finances before our children leave home. Those lessons include how to use a credit card and understand a paycheck.

LITTLE SPIES

Like highly trained CIA agents, our kids are studying us all the time—even when we think they're distracted. Sometimes it's shocking to hear them repeat our words back to us; sometimes it's adorable. One thing is for sure: In all things, from eating to getting dressed to interacting with our partners, we are their models. For better or for worse, they are basing their own budding identities on what they see us do. As Tori Spelling's therapist told her (during an episode of her reality TV show *True Tori*) as she tried to rebuild her marriage, our kids will grow up to be exactly like us. So if you want them to be healthy and happy (and wealthy), change yourself first.

As two-year-olds, my kids started pretending to go to the grocery store by carrying little tote bags around our house, picking up toys, and putting them inside the bags. When it came time to pay for the items at the pretend cash register (my hand), they would slap their pretend credit cards into my hands. "There you go!" they called. They've pretty much only seen me and their dad paying for anything with plastic or online. It made us think twice, so now we pull out cash more often instead of our credit cards, so our kids can start to grasp the concept that money is real. I also make sure that both my son and daughter see me paying for items at the store or picking up the bill at restaurants, even though it means I have to fight the urge to just let my husband always pick up the check.

After my conversation with Judith Ward at T. Rowe Price, I started looking for ways to make it easier for both my kids to watch some of my daily money decisions. When my daughter needed a gymnastics leotard, we scrolled through the different options online together and compared prices. At the grocery store, I showed her how to look at the per unit price for making apples-to-apples price comparisons when milk cartons come in different sizes, as I remember my dad teaching me. At the school book fair, I told her that her budget was $20, and when she reached it, she understood that she couldn't get another book, even though she wanted one.

So much about money today is invisible or at least so highly conceptual that hands-on demonstrations can be challenging. How can I easily explain to my kids that I opened up a 529 account for them for college savings when it was all done through a website? How can I explain a mortgage payment and the cable bill when both are automatically deducted from our bank account every month? Or that their dad and I automatically deduct money from our paychecks into our 401(k)s every paycheck? From the research from T. Rowe Price, Charles Schwab, and others, I knew that we had to be having these conversations; I just wasn't sure exactly how.

I ended up copying a strategy from my favorite parenting expert—my mom. She wrote a letter to my two younger sisters and me just as we were entering adulthood, detailing the financial choices that she and my dad made and explaining how certain frugal choices allowed them to buy a house and save for our educations. She shared how she and my dad saved a quarter of their relatively modest incomes when they first got married, which allowed them to buy a small house before I was born. She also explained that they made avoiding credit card debt a priority.

Her letter had come to me just as I was making big decisions of my own: whether to return to graduate school, what type of career to pursue, and whether to open a retirement account with my first, low-paid job. What she wrote wasn't surprising—I had grown up watching her make frugal choices all along—but it helped solidify my financial values and the approach I wanted to take with my money.

The letter also included a few things I did not know about; specifically, that my parents nearly had to borrow money from relatives early on in their marriage after a drunk driver hit them just as they were about to close on that first house. (That was before my mom had learned about the importance of an emergency fund.) My mom also shared her investing mistakes, including the time she put money into a product that lost money after all the adviser fees were paid. She finished off the missive with a list of action steps that reads like one of the personal finance articles I now write on a daily basis: Start saving for retirement early, be wary of financial advisers that push products on you while earning fees for doing so, and never invest in anything you don't understand.

Over the next several years, as I gained footing in my own financial life, earning steady income for the first time and starting to save for retirement, I ended up following almost all of her advice. Perhaps I would have done so anyway, having grown up absorbing lessons just by watching her, but her letter put many of those values into words and gave me something I can reread whenever I need a refresher.

TALKING POINTS

If you are like most parents, the idea of sitting down and talking about money with your kids is about as appealing as broaching where babies come from with a preschooler or safe sex with a teen. It's awkward and uncomfortable. But it is also just as important, because our kids' futures will be greatly impacted by what they learn from us.

The 2011 Charles Schwab Teens and Money survey found that 82 percent of teens say they learned to manage money from their parents, and three in four believe their parents have been great role models, but they are hungry for more: The surveyed teens said they would like to learn more about insurance, investing, income taxes, and savings strategies. They also said they want their parents to talk more about budgeting and managing credit with them.

In that spirit, here are a dozen conversations to consider having with your kids—dependent, of course, on their age and customized according to life experiences and family culture. They are based on my interviews with mothers, financial literacy experts, and researchers on how kids learn and what they need to come of age in our complicated financial world.

NO. 1:

MISTAKES YOU'VE MADE WITH MONEY

Young kids love to hear about the mistakes you've made. It not only makes you seem a bit less infallible, but it lets them know that it's okay to make mistakes if even their parents aren't perfect. Potential examples that you can share include waiting to start a 401(k) account, getting into credit card debt, not saving enough, and wasting money on a splurge you didn't really need.

NO. 2:

HOW YOU EARN MONEY
(AND USE IT TO PAY FOR FAMILY EXPENSES)

The fact that our paychecks are so often direct-deposited—and that we make so many purchases online or with plastic—has made the exchange of goods and services for cash almost invisible. My children think Amazon is a vast land of items that anyone can have sent to them with a few clicks of a button. Talking about how Mom and Dad work hard to earn a paycheck so that we can turn around and use it to pay for our food, home, and car is one way to make the virtual world of commerce a little more real.

As they get older, kids can start to understand more about the various ways people earn money and the importance of being entrepreneurial in today's economy. A look at the handmade shops on Etsy could interest a fourteen-year-old who loves crafting or making art. With your help, she could even start her own shop. (Be sure to encourage your daughters to find ways to earn money as much as your sons. The Charles Schwab teen survey found that even as teens, boys are already outearning girls— earning $1,880 compared to $1,372.)

NO. 3:

HOW TO BE A MEDIA CRITIC

I couldn't believe it when as a four-year-old, my daughter started getting excited about ads shown briefly before otherwise educational programming. "We need that!" she would tell me as the screen flashed with a colorful toy. Young children don't yet have the ability to view ads critically or tell the difference between an ad and a show, so as parents, we have to shield them and, as they get older, teach them how to be skeptical of all the promises that advertising makes.

The nonprofit Common Sense Media has found that kids are exposed to advertising everywhere: smartphone apps, websites, and even product placements within children's TV shows. Those ads can have a serious negative impact on children, including body images issues and even eating disorders, according to the organization. A study from University of Arizona found that the advertisements kids are exposed to as children can continue to affect them into adulthood, leading them to be drawn to sugary cereals, for example. Given the power of ads on kids' brains, I try to avoid letting my children see them, and plan to talk more critically about them as they get older. (I also use Common Sense Media's rating system for movies and other kids' entertainment to try to avoid programming that is filled with consumerism, as well as violence and inappropriate sexual content.)

NO. 4:

ECON 101

Even if you are a little fuzzy on some of these high-level concepts yourself, there are books that help make learning (or reviewing) together fun. For eight- to fourteen-year-olds, the novel *How Ella Grew an Electric Guitar,* by finance professor Orly Sade (with writer Ellen Neuborne), is a great introduction to economic concepts and entrepreneurship. The author was inspired by her life at home: Her then-fourth-grade daughter wanted to start a business and Sade couldn't find a book that would help her get started, so she decided to write one. Another good book for middle-schoolers, focused more on investing, is Elissa Weissman's *The Short Seller.* The protagonist figures out how to sell stocks online while she's home sick from school.

NO. 5:

PLANNING FOR BIG GOALS

When kids start asking for expensive things, as kids tend to do, you can encourage them to draw a picture of what they want and consider different ways the family could save to make that goal possible. It gets them thinking about trade-offs and delayed gratification. One of the biggest goals for the family might be saving for college, and when your kids start asking about it, you can explain how you are making sacrifices to put money toward their education.

NO. 6:

PRACTICING GENEROSITY AND GRATITUDE

Families vary greatly on their attitudes and practices toward giving. I spoke with some parents who tithe 10 percent of their income to their religious institution while others give more sporadically throughout the year, writing checks for school charity fundraisers whenever asked. One common theme that I found myself drawn to for my own family was to incorporate some kind of gratitude practice into daily life, whether it's stopping to show appreciation for a meal or talking about what you appreciated or are grateful for in a weekly family meeting. (Something my own family did when I was growing up.)

The point is to take a break from wanting and to appreciate what we do have, which cultivates a feeling of richness in itself and also gives an opportunity to consider how we might be able to help others who are not as fortunate.

NO. 7:

FRUGAL HABITS

I like the visual idea that *New York Times* columnist Ron Lieber proposes in his book on how to raise money-smart kids, *The Opposite of Spoiled*. He recommends that you draw a line labeled "needs" on one side and "wants" on the other, and write down different items along that spectrum. When your kids next make a request, they can consider where it belongs on that line.

NO. 8:

PRIVACY PROTECTION ONLINE

Protecting privacy defends not just our kids' financial futures, but also their safety. When they first start to go online, we can explain to them how to limit personal details and the photos that they share, because whatever they post is potentially accessible to strangers and searchable online forever. We can show them how to keep personal data like birth dates offline and even how to use fake names with online accounts. That's what online privacy expert and author Julia Angwin encourages her own children to do. That way, their friends know who they are online but they are anonymous otherwise. (It's the same strategy used by health professionals who don't want patients finding their personal Facebook accounts.)

NO. 9:

FINANCIAL TOOLS THAT PROTECT YOU FROM UNFORTUNATE EVENTS

Even teenagers might find this topic a bit dry—I know I didn't listen to my mom's lectures about the importance of wills and life insurance until I was a parent myself. Nonetheless, it can be useful to emphasize to risk-seeking teens that as twentysomethings, they'll want to make sure they have certain protections in place, like renter's insurance and health insurance.

NO. 10:

HOW TO USE CREDIT CARDS AND BANK ACCOUNTS

Even with the frequent conversations my parents had with me about money, this one fell through the cracks. That's why on a trip off campus during my college days I stood at the ATM for five minutes, with impatient customers lined up behind me, trying to figure out how the heck to insert my debit card and get money out of the machine. A few months later, I realized I had overdrawn my bank account and had to pay a penalty fee. It's not the worst way to learn, and I never overdrew my accounts again, but the situation might have been prevented with a few hands-on trips to the bank as a teen.

Similarly, it's not at all obvious that you should really try to pay off the full credit card balance each month as opposed to paying the required minimum. Letting kids look over your shoulder as you manage your accounts and pay your bills can implant some of these lessons.

NO. 11

BEING ASSERTIVE (TO COMPANIES AND BOSSES)

Let your kids overhear you calling a company to ask for a refund or to demand better service; show your kids how it's done because they may have to do the same one day, too. Similarly, help your kids practice asking for more money before they get their first salary offer so that they can learn the right words to use and can get comfortable with the concept of negotiation. And as we know, girls in particular can benefit from this encouragement.

My dad held this practice conversation with me the night before I negotiated my first job salary, and the subsequent conversation ended up netting me a starting salary that was $5,000 higher than it would have been if I hadn't asked. Since all future salaries were based on that first one, my dad's guidance has already boosted my take-home pay by well over $100,000. Research by Linda Babcock and Sara Laschever, authors of *Women Don't Ask*, estimates that women who negotiate their salaries earn $1 million or more over their careers compared to women who don't.

NO. 12:

GETTING COMFORTABLE WITH RETIREMENT AND INVESTMENT CONCEPTS

Getting teens familiar with terms like 401(k)s and Roth IRAs can help get them ready to open up their first retirement accounts when they land their first job as twentysomethings. We can help ease young people's fears of the stock market by talking about it and even showing them our own retirement profiles when they're ready.

What's surprising is how easily these conversations come up once you start looking for opportunities to have them. As I worked on this chapter, I started noticing the chance to talk about money with my daughter almost every day. When my office hosted a toy drive, I explained to her why we needed to pick an unopened toy to donate to a child who did not have any toys. When it was time for us to work on our taxes while she and her brother watched a movie, my husband and I gave her a brief overview of why a portion of our income goes toward paying for government services. A question about why I didn't have a car when I was a teenager led to an extended discussion about the cost of gas and insurance as well as the expense of a car itself. We also started noticing more financial topics embedded in the books we were reading, including Beverly Cleary's Ramona series, especially after Ramona's father loses his job and has to find a new one. Both of my children also love Vera B. Williams's *A Chair for My Mother,* about saving change for buying a new chair after a house fire. The visual effect of storing up leftover change in a giant jar makes sense to them.

Every time my daughter asks for a story from "when I was a little girl," a daily request on the car trip to school, I try to incorporate stories about how my parents taught us not to waste any food and what it was like for my father—her grandfather—to grow up with rations during post–World War II England. (She soon started asking him directly to regale her with stories of only being allowed to use a certain amount of hot water in baths and why his parents grew their own vegetables in a "victory garden" in their backyard.)

Grandparents, in fact, have a key role to play when it comes to these money talks. In a 2014 TIAA-CREF survey of over 1,000 grandchildren and their grandparents, three in four respondents said their grandparents influenced their saving and spending habits—but only three in ten grandparents realized it. The researchers pointed out that grandparents' stories about growing up during lean times or experiencing hardship can help to open their grandchildren's eyes to thriftier ways and a less materialistic culture than the one they know.

The biggest takeaway for me from my talks with other moms was that as parents, we can't be passive about our kids' financial educations, and especially when it comes to our daughters. As with lessons about healthy eating or safe sex, parents have to take charge of the conversation or kids will start to pick up all sorts of false and even harmful ideas. Between advertising on television and the seemingly magical powers of Amazon Prime, my kids could easily lose a sense of limits and frugality. Left untended, I could imagine unhealthy, wasteful behaviors taking root, from buying books and toys as soon as they are desired to a sense of entitlement without any generosity or responsibility attached.

I knew that some of my conversations were sinking into my five-year-old's head, because she started bringing up the topic herself. She will now remind us that we shouldn't go out to lunch because it's too expensive. She has even sweetly offered to give us all of her savings in the event that we ever run out of money. When I sat down to pay bills one weekend morning, she asked if she could help me. She sat beside me and watched as I tried to figure out why our water bill had gone up so much from the previous period, and then explained to her dad that we had to look for ways to waste less water. (She most enjoyed helping put the stamp and return address on the envelope.) When her little brother almost ruined our sofa by drawing all over it with a silver crayon, she was even more upset than her parents, since "buying a new sofa would be too expensive." (She also worked as hard as we did to scrub the crayon marks off.)

SCHOOLS OF THOUGHT

Each time I asked smart moms—and dads—how they handled allowances in their families, I heard a different yet specific method, highly tailored based on their kids' personalities, preferences, and family history. No two allowance plans were identical, but each seemed to work well for the family that invented it. And most parents—70 percent, according to a 2015 T. Rowe Price survey—opt to give their children some kind of an allowance.

Steve Schaffer, founder and CEO of the coupon and deal site Offers.com, gives each of three school-age children $5 plus 50 cents for every year of their age, so his youngest, a ten-year-old, gets $10. Then, they pay 25 percent of that money toward what Steve calls "family taxes." For the ten-year-old, that leaves $7.50. She then has to put 15 percent into a savings account and give 10 percent to charity, and the rest can be spent however she wants. (His wife keeps careful track of the amounts on index cards.) All three kids pooled their charity funds one year to give another child a bike for Christmas. They end up using their spending money for little luxuries they want, like toys, although Steve says that he's already noticed that they are thinking through trade-offs differently. His son initially wanted an iPhone, but after learning how much the monthly expenses would be, he opted to wait until he was older. "It's about teaching them the value of a dollar," he says.

In *The Opposite of Spoiled,* Lieber writes that after he gives his daughter her allowance in cash each week (he recommends starting out at 50 cents to $1 per year of age), she divides it into three different containers, for spending, giving, and saving. Instead of a piggy bank, which is rarely transparent and contains a subtle message that saving money is piggish, she uses decorated clear plastic containers for cash storage. Then, if she wants something on vacation or at the toy store, she can turn to her "spending" container and figure out what she can afford. While his daughter has certain responsibilities around the house, he's careful not to tie allowance money to chores because he says doing so implies that chores constitute voluntary paid work instead of mandatory "pitching in" around the house. (The T. Rowe Price survey found that 85 percent of parents do connect chores or some other type of household responsibility to allowance money.)

Writer and financial literacy advocate Alisa Weinstein wanted to use her family allowance system to show her children, ages seven and ten, how enjoyable work can be. She pays them an allowance based on their completion of assignments related to potential future careers, like creating a brochure as a travel agent or making a fingerprint log as a police officer. Separately, they are responsible for completing family chores, like making their beds. She says it teaches her kids that "this is how Mommy and Daddy earn money in the real world." Weinstein, who lives in the Washington, D.C. area, wrote her book, *Earn It, Learn It*, to help other parents copy her career-based system.

Carrie Smith, a financial blogger, told me that in her blended family, her father and stepmother took extra steps to make sure the allowance system was fair to Carrie, her three younger siblings, and her stepbrother. They paid each child an allowance every week and matched the money they put into savings to go toward their first car purchases as well as college tuition. They also frequently talked about spending, saving, and budgeting along the way. "We had regular family talks about our goals and where our family was at financially. My dad always told us when our family was lean with money a certain month, and that we had to think about our spending more carefully," Carrie recalls. If there was a school or sports event, they had to plan and save for it. Then, when she saved $8,000 for her first car purchase, her father matched it, which let her purchase a 2003 Jeep Liberty.

When I was growing up, long before my mom's detailed letter on financial management arrived, my parents used a similar matching system to encourage me and my two younger sisters to save. For every dollar we directed into our bank accounts from our allowance money, they matched the amount, up to $100. After $100, they matched half. That system allowed me to pay for a trip to Australia as a freshman in college, a lesson on the joy of delayed gratification that I'll never forget.

As I conducted my allowance research, I soon realized that the haphazard way my husband and I were paying our daughter an allowance—giving her a quarter every time she cleans the living room—wasn't working. She wasn't learning anything about saving or budgeting. We have since decided to institute a more formal system instead. Now she has chores to do around the house, including cleaning her room and emptying silverware out of the dishwasher, and separately, she gets $1 every Saturday to put in her piggy bank. (We are thinking of switching to a clear plastic container instead, as Lieber suggests.) She can choose to spend that money as she wants at the toy store or to buy souvenirs on our next family trip to the beach. As she gets older, our system will evolve to become more complex and we'll incorporate our children more into our charitable giving decisions, but for now, this works for us.

While every family's allowance system is different, the successful ones tend to have certain elements in common. They incorporate different categories for spending, saving, and giving; they grant freedom to spend the "spending money" however the child wants; they allow a regular disbursement of funds once a week. They also require a system for tracking and storing the money so that it is not forgotten or lost, such as virtually through index cards or tucked into some type of easily accessible container. Savings matching is used to provide extra incentive to delay gratification, and there are constant conversations and updates to the allowance system as needs evolve and children grow.

SMART MOM, RICH MOM
ACTION STEPS

1. Consider the financial behavior you are currently modeling for your children and what you might want to change to send a different message. Do they see you paying for goods and services that bring you pleasure? Do they watch you opt to hold off on other purchases or delay them? Do they see you making trade-offs or talking through financial choices?

2. Look for ways to have more conversations about money with your kids, even if they are still young. Use opportunities that come up naturally from the ques-

tions your kids ask, whether it's about being faced with a purchasing decision or explaining why you are paying bills.

3. If you have a spouse or partner, think about what your kids observe about the way that you manage money together. Is one person usually the one paying or handling bills and making financial decisions? If your financial responsibilities fall along gender lines, you might want to consider making things more equitable, not just for your own financial future but for your children's education.

4. Enlist the support of extended family members, especially grandparents, who can help make frugal lessons feel more real with stories of their own childhoods. If they live far away, encourage your children to ask them questions about their lives through Skype calls or emails.

5. Design an allowance system that makes sense for your family, based on the histories, ages, and preferences of your kids and their current habits. You might want to experiment with the different methods mentioned in this chapter before settling on a custom approach.

6. Put a voice to your family financial values through a letter written to your children or a jointly written family mission statement, which highlights goals, priorities, and values. (The handbook in the back of the book offers a "Dear Daughter" letter as a template to get started.)

7. Seek help where you need it to help flesh out your child's financial education. Plenty of resources exist for parents who want to teach their kids more about money. Private financial institutions offer kid-friendly sites, such as T. Rowe Price's MoneyConfidentKids. com. The government offers several online resources at MyMoney.gov, MoneyasYouGrow.org, and Admongo. gov. And a site from the Corporation for Public Broad- casting, pbskids.org/dontbuyit, will help you create budding media critics.

9

BACK TO YOU

While parenting certainly never ends—I know I still need my mom, even as a mom myself—there is a point where it eases up a bit. It might happen slowly, or all at once when your youngest heads to college, but at some point, you have as much time for yourself again as you did before becoming a mom. With a little luck and planning, you also have the life experience and resources to invest in yourself and explore new beginnings. You can think about what you want to do next, and even who you want to be, now that raising children doesn't eat up every moment of the day and every ounce of your energy. (And if you're still in the cyclone of the sippy cup and diaper years, trying to get everything done during naptime, you can find a glimpse of your here-before-you-know-it future in this chapter, and learn how to prepare for it.)

However you decide to fill your new free time, it has financial ramifications. Perhaps you'll elect to work harder at your job, increasing your income and retirement nest egg. Maybe you have visions of the opposite, scaling back so that you can take on more volunteer work, shift fields altogether, start something new, or perhaps return to a long-forgotten hobby. It might be time to go back to school, get training in something wildly different from what you've done for the last few decades, or open up a business.

At American University's School of Professional and Extended Studies, I teach a class on social media tailored to women at midlife who are going through some kind of transition. They often sign up just as their children are leaving for college, or when their marriages have dissolved, or when they're seeking to change their careers. (Sometimes they are experiencing all three upending life events at once.) They have usually signed up for my class because they want their social media presence to reflect their new and shifting identities and support their next steps. They have taught me so much about how to prepare for midlife and retirement, from choices they made and didn't make.

One woman, a former scientist who left her high-powered full-time job to raise her daughters fifteen years ago, is now leveraging her science background for a new career in a beauty product franchise. She hopes to earn a steady income again as a self-employed entrepreneur who sets her own hours, since her children still live at home. Another divorced mom of two is reviving her freelance writing and producing career, which she last did full-time before having children. Another empty-nester mom, who lost her husband to cancer, is slowly building a more creative career in copywriting and blogging, moving away from the customer relations work she had been doing. All are balancing their life choices with their financial needs, preferences, and limitations.

Through one of my students, I met Maryam Amini, a fifty-one-year-old divorced mom of two twentysomething children who has newly launched a real estate career. As Maryam drove from her Long & Foster office back to her new apartment in suburban Washington, D.C., she explained that after separating from her husband, she needed to earn her own income. While her children were young, she was primarily a stay-at-home mom, although she took on some part-time work in bookkeeping and event organizing. "Right now I'm getting alimony, and I'm frightened every day he's going to cut it. I want to be able to work and make myself 100 percent independent, which I've never done before. I'm determined to do it—I owe it to myself," she says.

She chose real estate as her next career move partly because instead of discriminating against women as they age, she says it values their maturity. "The older you are, people trust you more. You need some life experience to advise people on such a big investment," she says. She also likes the flexibility of the schedule. "I want freedom at this stage of my life to travel and make my own schedule." Her first client is herself and her ex-husband— she's selling the home they lived in as they raised their family. She plans to use the open houses and other events related to the sale to market herself and pick up more clients.

While the divorce and its financial ramifications have been stressful, causing many sleepless nights, Maryam says she now feels more excited about her future than ever:

I feel so powerful and independent and I've never felt this before. I can stand up for myself. At fifty-one, I've accomplished something, and look forward to a future. A couple years ago, I thought life was over, that I would just go into my hole and stay there. Now, it's a new life for me. I look forward to everything. I get up and it's a new day.

Moms like Maryam are at the peak of what the anthropologist Margaret Mead dubbed "postmenopausal zest" in the 1950s. Gail Sheehy dedicated one of her bestsellers, *The Silent Passage,* to the topic, writing that menopause can bring new energy and life to women's lives. Celebrity doctor Christiane Northrup argues that the stage can coincide with new levels of creativity, ambition, and a desire to serve others in the community.

How we choose to do that has a big impact on our financial standing. If we keep working, delaying Social Security until we reach full retirement age, then we can not only find new purpose in our work, but can also continue bringing in income. If we launch a business, we might continue running it into our seventies or eighties. Or, we can leverage the wealth that we have been building over our lifetimes and use it to invest in new classes or experiences, or to become more actively engaged in volunteer or charity work.

The moms I interviewed pursued all sorts of directions for this stage of their lives, and their choices contain many lessons for those of us who are still years and even decades away from retirement. As the career research done by professors Lisa Mainiero and Sherry Sullivan, mentioned in Chapter 4, suggests, midlife moms are often in deep pursuit of work that feels authentic to them. Change is often painful: They may be giving up a comfortable nine-to-five job that is no longer stimulating; taking a class in something that is far outside their comfort zone, like memoir writing; risking failure when they launched a new business.

As moms, we can prepare for this stage of life by beginning new ventures and exploring different paths even while young children are still at home. That might be possible by beginning a daddy-child outing tradition on Saturday afternoons so that you can stay home and write. Or it might mean sneaking out early Sunday mornings for a solo yoga class, just to have time to think. Many moms I spoke with opted to wake up early, before their children, or to stay up late, engaging in an activity that made them feel creatively alive, like running their Etsy shop or blogging. Taking care of yourself, and your ambition, is not only good for you, but it's good for your family, too.

THE MONEY QUESTIONS

Moms approaching this stage of life tend to be faced with some serious financial decisions. With retirement approaching and careers often in flux, moms are often asking themselves: What should I do with the wealth I have accumulated so far? How can I keep earning money as I age, especially if I want to slowly transition into retirement or have more control over my schedule? How can I afford to make my "big dream" happen, whether it's launching a business or spending three months in Paris? And how can I make up for prior money mistakes, from not saving enough to accumulating debt?

When I talked to both financial experts and midlife mamas about these financial crossroads, one common strategy that emerged was the importance of taking a much more active and conscious role in money management, especially for those who had been relatively hands-off until now. By your forties, you can already start to glimpse your financial future in retirement, and if it doesn't look secure, that's a scary wake-up call—enough to inspire some budgeting cuts today, if necessary. It's a good time to once again pull up the online retirement calculators (mentioned in Chapter 5) to make sure you're on track.

No matter what stage you're at, it is not too late to play catch-up for earlier savings lapses. If you haven't reached your retirement targets, now is the time to make up for that. Look for ways to cut your current costs so that you can slip the maximum annual amount into tax-advantaged retirement funds. Seek a risk profile that makes sense for your stage—if you only have a decade or two left until full retirement, then you'll want to be more conservatively invested than a thirtysomething mom with another thirty years of work ahead of her. You also want to make sure you have a solid emergency fund to cover six months' worth of expenses (or more); layoffs can happen at any age, and older adults generally have a harder time finding a new job when they do. Unexpected health care expenses are also more likely to pop up at this stage of life.

Hearing from older moms can often shed light—and provide inspiration—for making smarter choices today. When I put out a call on Twitter for "grandmothers available to talk money" with me, I immediately heard back from Kitt Turner, a sixty-year-old grandmother and bankruptcy attorney in Philadelphia. When I gave her a call at her office, she explained that she has a three-year-old grandson who is just starting to grasp the concept of needs versus wants. As an avid watcher of CNBC, she said she is considering giving him a share of Disney one day, so he can begin to understand the stock market.

As for her own finances, she explained, her biggest concern is if she's going to have enough money to last her the rest of her life. Like many moms, she wishes she had started saving more money for retirement earlier. Now, she's doing what she can to catch up to where she'd like to be.

"A few years ago, I started saying, 'Okay, how much money will I need to live in retirement?'" she says. She created three different budget levels, which she playfully dubbed her "cat food," "tuna," and "sushi" budget. She was hoping to save enough to achieve sushi-level budgeting, at least some of the time. Then, she started tracking all of her expenditures to see how much she was spending. "I realized I was leaking money all over the place," she says.

Thinking about how she spent in her twenties and thirties, she says, "I kick myself every day. I should have started much sooner." With her kids, she's constantly reminding them to put money into their 401(k)s so that they can benefit from compounding interest over the decades. Since she got serious about budgeting a few years ago, Kitt has started putting much more money away for retirement, but she'll always regret missing out on those years of potential compounding.

Kitt's plan now is to continue working as a bankruptcy attorney as long as possible, although she acknowledges that when to retire might not be entirely within her control. There's always the chance of jobs disappearing or illness striking. She hopes to keep working for at least six more years at the minimum, when she'll reach her full retirement age and can take Social Security payments without a penalty. Then, she plans to turn her energy to part-time work as an attorney, volunteering, and, of course, her grandson.

Working well past traditional retirement age is a theme I often heard from the moms I interviewed, especially if they had found work that they enjoyed and felt was meaningful. (It's not just moms, either. A 2012 Charles Schwab survey found that one in three middle-income workers in their sixties said they don't want to retire, with most saying that was by choice, not because they had to continue working for the money.) Working longer takes all different forms. It may mean starting up their own businesses later in life, taking a professional career part-time or going freelance so they have more control over their hours, or using the expertise they built up over a lifetime and applying it to volunteer work. That's the path my own mom has taken. After spending her career as a consumer advocate working on health care policy, she now is helping her town prepare itself to help residents age in place, by reducing isolation, organizing free rides to doctors, and helping people navigate their Medicare benefits.

If you can manage to delay receiving Social Security until your full retirement age, as Kitt Turner aims to do, then you will receive more money each month. It's like buying an annuity without all the fees and commissions. You "pay" with reduced income in your sixties and then benefit from the higher income later. If your full retirement age is 67, for example, as it is for anyone born in 1960 or later, then your benefits will be reduced by about 30 percent if you start taking them at age 62. The reduction goes down by a sliding scale the longer you wait to receive the benefit, until age 67, when you get the full benefit. If you delay further to age 70, your benefit will go up even more, by a percentage based on the year you were born. It's a great way to boost your quality of life in your later years—if you can afford the reduced income in your early sixties. (Of course, politicians debate raising the retirement age regularly, so it's possible the rules will change further before you see any money.)

SOMETHING NEW

Another recurring theme among the moms I interviewed is the importance of actively investing in what you want to do next, whatever that might be. Depending on the direction you want to move in, you might have to spend some money and time getting there. That could mean working with a career coach, taking a course at a local university, or getting a new certification in your field. While challenging, these investments can be especially grounding if you are also juggling another major transition, such as divorce, children going to college, or retiring from a full-time job.

If you have a partner, then you'll want to sit down for a chat about how you both see the next few decades unfolding: for example, how you want to spend and manage your money, when you want to stop working or if you want to work less, and how you want to spend your free time. When Ellen Rogin, a certified financial planner and coauthor of *Picture Your Prosperity*, talked with her husband about their retirement dreams, she was shocked to hear that he wanted to go on a big sailing trip to the Caribbean with friends. After almost three decades of marriage, she had never heard him say that before; they were able to start planning for it once they had that discussion.

Earning money through entrepreneurial pursuits is also a popular option for moms who have more freedom and time on their hands as their children become more independent. The extra money generated from those pursuits can also help fund big travel dreams or other splurges, as well as retirement.

When her daughter was a toddler, Dana Lisa Young, a wellness practitioner in Atlanta, decided to ramp up what was then her side business, practicing reflexology and serving as a life coach to clients, and eventually left her full-time content management job at a professional services firm. Not only did she gain more control over her schedule, but she also felt more creative and professional satisfaction. "I love being able to help people learn how to prioritize self-care and improve their physical and emotional well-being. It's very fun, rewarding, and inspiring work seeing people's lives change for the better," she says. She sets her own hours and does most of her client work during the school day and sometimes in the early evenings, when her husband is home, as well as part of Saturdays. Dana, now in her mid-forties, continues to build her business, teaching more workshops and leading retreats, while also working on a book about healing.

Author and mom Lynne Strang made a similar move at midlife, when her children were grown. She had spent almost three decades as a communications executive when she decided to leave office life behind and embark on a freelance writing career. Her children were in high school when she made the transition; she says she craved flexibility in her schedule even more than she did when they were younger. She was tired of her two-hour round-trip commute and wanted to take on more volunteer work, too. "I wasn't looking to work fewer hours, but I wanted to have more control over when and where I worked those hours," she says.

She turned in her notice and embarked on a career as a freelance writer and consultant. She had to take a pay cut, but because she had always lived below her means, opened retirement accounts early on in her career, maxed out her 401(k) contributions every year she held a traditional job, and avoided credit card debt, she was able to transition to a new lifestyle without major hiccups. Her first project was writing a book about other entrepreneurs who got their start later in life. She published her book, *Late-Blooming Entrepreneurs: 8 Principles for Starting a Business After Age 40*, while also helping her teenage children navigate high school and college applications. "As they get older, they continue to need support from their parents, but the type of support they need changes," she says. While her kids were young and she was focused on climbing the corporate career ladder, she had her parents and in-laws nearby to help provide the kind of hands-on care young children need. Now, she has more time for her grown children—and herself.

GETTING MORE SOCIAL

If building a new career or professional identity—or even just further developing the one you already have—is part of your plan, then social media platforms can help you do that. They play an increasingly important role in the financial and career worlds, as more companies and people embrace them as their favored forms of communication with the wider world. Whether intentionally or not, social media projects who you are—what you're good at, what interests you, what you have to offer—into the world. That impacts the types of jobs and opportunities that come your way, whom you meet professionally and personally, and even whether you are likely to be the target of a scam artist.

While there's certainly a creepy side to the fact that people can quickly learn details about you online, like the value of your home, which is readily available to anyone who knows your address, it can also be a powerful tool for getting what you want, especially as your goals shift over time. You can define yourself however you want to online and use the platforms to reach out to potential employers or clients. If you've been a copyeditor your whole life and want to transition to being a writer, you can call yourself a writer on your Twitter profile and start pitching articles to websites or magazines. If you've been a stay-at-home mom and now you're launching your own Etsy business, your Twitter ID can feature the words "creative entrepreneur" with a link back to your Etsy shop. You can join Twitter chats on Etsy about creative entrepreneurship. Your social media accounts can serve as arrows, gently pointing you in the direction you want to go until you get there.

One of my students wanted to be an activist on behalf of students speaking English as a second language as part of her teaching career. She listed #ESOL as one of her interests on her Twitter profile; started sharing news about education, language, and immigration; and followed other leaders in that field. She started posting relevant articles on her Twitter page, followed immigration Twitter discussions using the hashtag #immigrationaction, and also made sure her LinkedIn profile reflected her interests, so potential employers and fellow activists could connect with her. She found her community online, and it could now find her.

Having a powerful, professional online presence can lead to opportunities that you wouldn't even have known existed otherwise. If you are a mom blogging about healthy family meals, then a health food company could ask you to be their spokesperson. If your name comes up when a recruiter searches for family lawyers in your town, then you could get yourself a new job opportunity or big client. If you are a photographer with a special skill in capturing outdoor family moments, then your Instagram feed could land you a steady stream of new clients when your current ones share it with their friends. Conversely, if someone runs a web search on your name and nothing comes up, or random things like a political donation disclosure turns up, or, even worse, an eighteen-year-old with your name and a penchant for partying and tweeting turns up, then you could lose an opportunity before you even knew it existed. Robin Fisher Roffer, author of the personal branding book *Make a Name for Yourself,* says that her online accounts help her set higher fees for her speaking engagements and also generate many of her clients for consulting services or webinars.

In addition to the financial benefits, there are social and even health benefits: According to the Pew Research Center's Internet and American Life Project, using social media can lower women's stress levels because it helps us feel supported and connected to others. You can share your goals with friends, get quicker customer service from retailers, and even ask your bank questions, all over Twitter or Facebook.

There are risks, too, though, and we can take steps to protect ourselves and our families—even after we're gone—from being hurt by what we have shared online. Just as scam artists browse the times of funeral services to prey on empty houses, they also prowl social media to pick up key information, like birth dates and anniversaries, which they can use to hack into financial accounts. The security questions on bank accounts often overlap with what can be seen on our Facebook profiles, even by strangers we haven't friended: the high school we went to and our mother's maiden name, for example. Those details can be used to reset a password remotely and give an attacker unfettered access to our banking information, passwords, or, as happened to a handful of celebrities, naked photos.

To protect your money (and your family), consider taking these steps to bolster the protection on your social media accounts:

1. Where it's available, such as on Facebook and Google, set up two-step verification. That way, when someone tries to log in from an unfamiliar device, they will have to enter a second password sent to a mobile device. While it can be inconvenient when you're traveling and using new devices, this process makes it much harder for someone to guess your password and then log in without you.

2. Use hard-to-guess passwords. While it's difficult to keep track of the dozens of passwords needed to navigate modern life today, it's essential to your financial

security to use complex passwords on not just your financial accounts but also your social media accounts, because a breach could allow someone to collect personal information about you that could compromise your identity and even allow a hack into your bank or investment accounts. One trick is to use long passwords made up of sentences with numbers interspersed as well ("myf8voritecityisTokyo"). You can also use an encrypted tool like KeePass.info to remember many passwords for you.

3. Never click on hyperlinks in emails that appear to come from real accounts. The classic "phishing" scam involves a fraudster penning an email that appears to come from a familiar site, like Twitter or Facebook, but the embedded link in the email takes you to a fake site that asks for your password. If you enter it, then the bad guys have your information. Instead, type in web addresses into the browser yourself, so you know you're not going to a fake site. One downside to sharing recent purchases on Facebook or Twitter, as retailers increasingly invite us to do, is that it makes it easy for an attacker to craft a fake email following up on that order and asking for extra information. If we see an email about something we just ordered, we could easily be fooled into clicking on it.

4. Consider the long-term plan for your digital assets. As mentioned in Chapter 6, you want to make sure your social media accounts are protected after death, too. Facebook allows you to appoint a legacy

contact, for example, so someone else can manage or shut down your account on your behalf.

5. Don't friend strangers. Some scam artists make their business around impersonating "friends," so we are tricked into accepting their friend requests and consequently sharing personal information about ourselves with complete strangers. If you are dating online, the risks are even higher, because scam artists target those looking for romance. In fact, the FBI reports that in the last six months of 2014, consumers lost $82 million to romance-related scams. Before friending anyone on social media or Facebook, you can also run a Google image search to help you determine if the person is authentic—or if it's a scam artist using a stolen image. Another obvious red flag is when a "friend" asks you for money to help her through an emergency. Disturbingly common and often known as the "grandparent" scam, since so many grandparents fall for it, it is also a common strategy among romance-related scams. To prevent family members from falling for this one, adopt a family code word that no one else knows. If anyone truly needs money in an emergency, he or she should use the code word to let the other person know that it is real.

6. Limit revealing pictures. If you like to share sonograms, birth certificates, hospital bracelets, and other images that include names, addresses, and even Social Security numbers, learn how to black out or blur those details before posting them.

7. Review your privacy settings. Regularly review your
    settings, so you know who can view your posts and
    images on your Facebook and other social media ac-
    counts. You might want to consider limiting them to
    friends only, so even if another friend shares the
    photo, it is not visible to strangers.

The ramifications of our social media accounts go well beyond money, too. Social media defines our legacy, whether or not
we want it to. Distant relatives, great-grandchildren, and even
strangers might come across postings in the future, given the
likely power of future search engines. What story will your public postings tell? One of my students, whose sister unexpectedly
passed away at midlife, found some solace in being able to connect with her Pinterest account to see what books and movies she
had posted about. She says it even allowed her to feel like she was
having a new conversation with her sister after she died. Mother
and writer Lisa Bonchek Adams tweeted her journey with stage
4 breast cancer, creating a powerful community of women who
rallied behind her until she died; her accounts lived on in memo-
riam. She also used Twitter to start a movement with the hashtag
#mondaypleads, which she used to remind women to make doc-
tor's appointments that they've been putting off. Her legacy is
literally saving lives.

Given the power and reach of social media, working on your
accounts, especially during times of transition, like when you are
trying to reignite your career or shift into a new one, can lead to
an existential crisis. Before you even pick your Twitter handle or
write your first 140-character missive, you have to decide who

you are and who you want to be. Are you going to define yourself by the career you're in the middle of? as a mom? As the entrepreneur you soon hope to be? The answer might be all three. Your identity might be shifting so quickly that you have to update your description every few months—something I do myself and constantly urge my students to do. It's basic digital maintenance, which increasingly falls under the umbrella of financial management, since our online identities can have such a big impact on our finances and earning power.

Social media accounts offer a chance to define yourself—and your life—and to create new connections and opportunities that didn't exist before.

SMART MOM, RICH MOM
ACTION STEPS

1. During ebbs from the intensity of parenting, take some time to reflect on what you want over the coming years, especially as your children become more independent. Do you want to launch a different career, become a volunteer, or rediscover an old hobby or passion? Even if you are years away from the "empty nest" stage, you start to plan, prepare, and save for new possibilities now.

2. If you have a partner, you can talk about what you each want to do in the next third of your lives. Make sure you are on the same page and aware of each

other's goals and dreams, especially ones that will have a big impact on your finances.

3. Make up for past money mistakes by saving more money for retirement (max out your annual contributions) and pay off any credit card debt that still lingers.

4. Invest in yourself by taking classes, earning new certifications, or perhaps working with a career coach as you plan your next steps in your life and career.

5. Plan on delaying receiving Social Security as long as possible; if you can wait until you reach your full retirement age (i.e., age 66 for those born between 1943 and 1954; 67 for those born in 1960 or later) or, better yet, wait until age 70, you will have a higher payment later. The Social Security Administration publishes a booklet, "What Every Woman Should Know," which is available online at ssa.gov. It explains Social Security benefits and concerns common to women, including how divorce affects benefits and how to receive benefits on behalf of an elderly or disabled relative you are taking care of.

6. Consider continuing to work in some way, even after retirement. This is a strategy that will also make it easier to delay receiving Social Security. Turning a previous side business into a consulting or coaching business, or transitioning from a full-time career into a consultant, may delay the need to tap into retirement savings and enhance your lifestyle.

7. Cultivate your online presence and social media accounts so that they reflect your goals for what you

want to do next. Buy the domain name for the blog or website that you've always wanted to launch. Make sure your LinkedIn account is filled out with details about your current and past jobs and use profession-al-looking photos to project who you want to be and who you are. If you are in job-seeking mode, look at how other leaders in your field represent themselves on LinkedIn and other social media platforms and consider applying some of the best practices to your own account. Then, when a hiring manager looks you up, you'll be one step closer to landing the job.

8. Protect your privacy (and your children's privacy) on-line. Scam artists prowl social media sites looking for vulnerable victims in order to commit financial fraud, which can empty out a savings account. Make sure de-tails that can be used to verify identity, like your birth date, are invisible to strangers, and never "friend" someone you don't know on Facebook. Review your list of Facebook friends at least once a year to make sure you know everyone listed. Avoid posting photos while you are on vacation, as this announces that your home is currently empty. Conduct Facebook's privacy checkup regularly to look for updates and make sure you know what you are sharing publicly. Don't post specific details about your finances; even sharing that you haven't yet filed your taxes as the tax deadline approaches can trigger a scam artist to file a fraudu-lent return in your name.

10

RETURNING TO
THE NEST

As your children get older and start building their own lives,
you might find that they boomerang back into your house
for a little bit. In fact, a 2015 report from the Pew Research
Center found that 26 percent of millennials, defined as between
the ages of 18 and 34, now live with their parents. This movement back home can be a wonderful time for everyone involved:
Kids get to live in a home that is usually far nicer than anything
they can afford; parents get to hang out with their children once
they are long past the diapers and tantrums stage, and this time
the kids can help out with chores, cooking, and paying some bills.
Even if your own children are still depending on you to pack their
lunch boxes every day and the idea of independence feels eons off,
knowing what's in store can help you prepare for it.

Plenty of research shows that this critical young adult period
is not unlike the fourth trimester of pregnancy, when newborns
are out of your body but unable to hold up their heads or do anything for themselves. Even after your children appear independent

on paper, they still need you for guidance, shelter, and possibly even food. If you help them, you can set them on a stronger path for the rest of their lives.

Barbara Ray, coauthor of the 2010 book *Not Quite Adults*, points out that research suggests a large divide between those whose parents can help them find their footing and those who are left to fend for themselves. Young adults who are forced to take the first job offered to them might "never really get ahead," she says. Parental assistance, on the other hand, can offer them the freedom they need to find their way to a productive and financially secure path. If too much help is given, though, it can also hamper their path to independence.

The trick to both of you surviving this period with your finances (and relationship) still intact is talking openly, planning ahead, and making sure you're mutually benefiting from any shared living arrangements. Remember Katy Hewson, the social worker and mom of two from Chapter 3, who lived with her parents after her first child was born? One reason the arrangement worked out so well and for so long (Katy and her family still live near her parents, although they no longer share a roof) is because her parents benefited, too, and not just because they got to spend so much time with their grandchildren.

When I asked Cindy Smith, Katy's mom, how she felt about their living arrangements, she explained that after Katy and her family moved to the suburbs, she and her husband, Gary, decided to sell their Houston home and move into the same suburban community as Katy, which conveniently is also nearby their son and his family. While they were living farther apart, Cindy says, "They missed us a lot," including the help with prepared dinners and babysitting. And Cindy and Gary missed being so close, too, especially to the youngest members of their family.

In their new home in the same community as their son, daughter, and their families, their grandchildren can walk to school and enjoy walks by the nearby lake. "It is an ideal situation for us," Cindy says. If her children decide to move again, she and Gary will probably be close behind, she says. "We can follow them wherever," she says. Meanwhile, she and Gary are traveling the world, taking cruises, and volunteering. "Our retirement years are wonderful," she says. When I emailed her to get a final update before this book's publication, she wrote me back from Australia, where she and Gary were on a cruise. "A well-planned retirement and a great partner are an awesome blessing," she wrote.

Even if you are not as physically close to your adult children as the Smiths are, and are just helping out with moral (or financial) support from a distance, conversations about money can still pay off, for both of you. Carrie Schwab-Pomerantz, senior vice president of Charles Schwab and author of *The Charles Schwab Guide to Finances After Fifty,* says she helped her twenty-something sons settle into their financial lives by helping them set up their 401(k)s. Both of her sons live in San Francisco, where they grew up and Carrie and her husband still live, and where housing costs are high. After one son got his first job, Carrie says, "I talked to him about creating a budget. He took what he knew he was going to earn, minus taxes and minus savings, and figured out what he could afford in terms of an apartment. He made sure he was saving in his 401(k)."

Retirement talk wasn't a new concept to any of her children

(she also has a daughter, who was in high school at the time of our conversation), but Carrie still thought it was worthwhile to sit down with them and go over their new job benefits and help them choose their investments for their retirement accounts. That packet of human resources paperwork when you get a new job is overwhelming, especially when it's your first one.

Many moms with grown children are still intimately involved in their children's lives—driving them to college, supporting them financially, monitoring their Facebook posts like supportive fans—but they are also consciously nudging them out of the nest. By talking to them about budgeting and saving, encouraging them in their job searches, and offering babysitting or cooking services when it means spending time together, they are gently sending their kids the message that they are ready to stand on their own, especially with their mom's (and often dad's) hands nearby ready to offer much-needed assistance. They also protect their own finances during this extended "adultescence" stage: According to TD Ameritrade's 2015 Financial Disruptions survey, one in four adults who experienced a disruption to their long-term savings and retirement plans pointed to the burden of supporting others as the reason.

DOWNSIZING

To help cut back on daily living costs, some empty nesters opt to downsize their homes and unload many of the expensive possessions that saw them through their prime parenting years. As she entered her fifties, Mary Cassaday of Reston, Virginia, was tired of maintaining the large family home that she and her husband, Steve, raised their three sons in. It had a long driveway that needed shoveling every winter and a swimming pool that required constant upkeep. "I was done taking care of such a big house," Mary says. They sold their 8,000-square-foot home and moved into one less than half the size in nearby Reston. Now Mary can spend half the year in Florida, as she wants to, without worrying about finding a house sitter. "There's enough space for the kids, so they can come home, get on their feet, and move on," she says. Mary and her husband don't have to schedule, or pay for, all that upkeep of the larger home, and they made some money unloading much of their furniture through a company that handles estate sales.

Another mom, Lynne Martin, made a similar but more extreme choice: After she and her husband sold their California home, they became serial renters, all around the world, including London, Paris, Italy, and Argentina. Now in their early seventies, Lynne and her husband, Tim, are still enjoying what they call the "gypsy" lifestyle. They live on a budget of $6,000 per month, generated from investments, and also collect Social Security. It was saving earlier in their lives when their children were still at home, Lynne says, that allowed them to afford to hit the road as seniors. They also balance pricey city stays with more frugal destinations to stay within their budget. They're also still working on the road, as writers. They documented their adventures in a memoir, "Home Sweet Anywhere," and post updates on their blog, homefreeadventures.com.

Even if you plan to stay closer to home and your ideal retirement day involves your favorite chair, a book, and a cup of tea, you can still benefit financially from constantly decluttering as your children grow out of toys, books, and clothes. "When your home is streamlined and you have systems in place, you also are less likely to buy things that you don't need," says expert organizer and *Rightsize . . . Right Now!* author Regina Leeds. Taking the time to regularly toss and shred documents that steadily accumulate can make it easier to stay on top of your paperwork even before you downsize. You might also decide you're ready to part with old furniture or family items that have already served their purpose. You might even make some money by selling them. (If you go with an online sale on something like Craigslist, just be sure to meet potential buyers in a public place and always have someone with you when meeting strangers.)

To protect yourself against all of the challenges we discussed in Chapter 7 regarding aging parents—cognitive decline, scam artists, financial abuse—you also want to make sure that someone you trust knows how to manage your money for you in case you need help or are temporarily incapacitated. This power of attorney document can be on file with an attorney along with your will, health proxy, and other estate planning documents. When we are young parents, we create these documents to protect our dependent children—but it's us who become the vulnerable ones as we age.

As with all transitions, aging brings up complicated decisions and emotions, and sometimes a financial professional who can offer an outside, unbiased perspective can help. We often become even more conservative with our investments as we age, hesitating to take risks that would allow us to stay ahead of inflation, especially if we're lucky enough to live to see our nineties.

MATRIARCHAL POWERS

It's easy to miss being young. I feel it most acutely when I'm stuck in traffic after work, rushing to make it to preschool pickup on time, and I catch sight of seemingly carefree local college students walking out of a hot yoga class, with iced coffees in hand. They look so fit, so relaxed, so . . . young. In weak moments, I envy them.

But then I remember what age has brought me. The infinite love for my children. The security of family. The ability to earn a paycheck that is bigger than it was in my twenties. The self-knowledge to know my own preferences for how to spend my time, dollars, and energy, and the willingness to say "no" to the things that don't fit into them. I wasted a lot of money and time in my twenties, buying things that didn't really mean much to me, attending parties I didn't really want to go to, and spending time with people who did not bring me joy. The older I get, the more I realize how short life is, and I value my own limited resources. More responsibilities, at both work and home, also require being pickier about how I spend those resources. (TV Land's *Younger*, starring Hilary Duff and Sutton Foster, explores this dynamic so insightfully as Foster's forty-year-old character pretends to be in her mid-twenties, finding aspects of the hipster lifestyle—dodgeball, being an entry-level employee, CrossFit workouts—so exhausting along the way. Sometimes, she just wants to embrace her age, staying home to watch *Downton Abbey* under a blanket with a glass of wine—and so do I.)

Embracing our new identities as the financial matriarchs of

our families also opens up new possibilities. We set the stage, we define the terms, both for our own lives and the lives of those around us. Studying how older women you admire embrace their age and wisdom can be a great source of inspiration for how we want to live as we age, both financially and otherwise. Women about fifteen years older than you who share similarities, like a profession, can serve as the best inspiration. Study them, figure out what you admire about them, and pick aspects about their lives to strive to replicate, including their financial choices.

Likewise, whether or not you know it, you are the teacher and the role model for not only your children, but younger members of your community and anyone who knows you. Our children are our closest observers. They watch how we respond to disappointment and frustration and whether we are happy as we go off to work or highly stressed. They notice if we develop a new mole on our forearms.

That's why grandmothers like Kitt Turner talk to their grandchildren about money and investing and demonstrate how to pursue a life of meaning and joy while living within one's means. Knowing that we are the templates by which our children and grandchildren start to shape their own lives raises the stakes—and makes it even more important that we are taking care of ourselves, the way we hope they take care of themselves one day. We're setting up patterns that could last for generations.

Once, before I became a mom but after I had gotten married, I asked my mom if she ever felt sad about certain life events now being in the past: finding her life partner, raising children, seeing them graduate. Wasn't it kind of depressing, I asked her, that those things are over? That she won't experience them again? She smiled and told me, "I'm just grateful that I made it." Instead of feeling down that time was passing, she was happy and thankful that we were all here to make it to the next stage. That's something she taught me: gratitude for being here, for making it this far.

Aging, especially after your own children are past the constant care stage, offers a chance to be selfish again. In a way, it's like being twentysomething again, but this time, you know what you do with all that freedom.

SMART MOM, RICH MOM
ACTION STEPS

1. Plan for a future where you and your adult children can mutually help each other out financially. Perhaps you can help them navigate their first budget and open their first 401(k) account. Getting your kids independent, on a solid path, will also make it less likely that they will still be asking you for money when they're thirty (or older).

2. As you plan for and envision your retirement years, consider new living arrangements and their financial ramifications, including downsizing, moving, or traveling. Constantly prune your paperwork and clutter so that if you do downsize in the future, the task is more manageable.

3. Embrace your role as the family matriarch. Younger family members will increasingly look to you for financial guidance and leadership, and you can find inspiration and support from older women you admire.

EPILOGUE

MORE THAN MONEY

One Sunday night over burgers, my husband and I were talking about the logistics of our upcoming week. I was scheduled to teach an evening class on Tuesday, so I asked if he could pick up our two children at preschool, which is usually my responsibility.

"I can do it, but it will be hard to leave early," he said, sounding stressed. Since he usually has meetings that extend into early evenings, my request would mean having to duck out midmeeting.

Just as I was about to thank him and move on to less anxiety-producing subjects, our five-year-old daughter piped up. "We have to work and make money," she told us. She likes to resolve conflicts and will often step in to help us do so, whether it's over how to load the dishwasher or make scheduling adjustments.

"Thank you!" I said, thinking she was explaining my need to get to my class on time so that I could teach. "You're right, Mommy has to work and make money!"

"No, no, no," she said. That was not what she meant at all. "Daddy has to work! You have to come pick us up!"

So much for my goal of trying to explain that moms and dads both work to support families, I thought. Does she really think only Daddy's work matters?

I tried to explain that Mommy makes money too, and that money helps pay for the things we have and want, like food, our home, and her dance classes. She responded that Daddy makes the money for that. We continued discussing gender equality for a few brief moments before someone wanted more ketchup and then a new shirt. But I kept thinking about it later—does my daughter really hold such traditional ideas? If so, where did they come from? And how can I change them, so she knows that her future career, dreams, and earnings are just as important as her brother's?

To try to answer these questions, I turned to the past, to yellowed and frayed copies of *U.S. News & World Report* magazine. I figured articles on personal finance, especially ones that focused on women written in the 1950s and 1960s, would illuminate our old-fashioned beliefs and, I hoped, show how far we have come from those more traditional days, when husbands were the breadwinners, at least in middle-class homes. From there, I hoped to get some direction on what we still had to do to create a culture where girls and boys see their parents as financial equals.

Deep in the *U.S. News* archives, I found the May 16, 1958, issue with a surprisingly modern-sounding cover story: "What Every Woman Should Know About Money." The focus of the green and white cover with bold yellow block letters could appear on any women's magazine today, and in fact, it often does. A web search of that headline brings up dozens of articles published within the last several years.

The article itself, with a few notable exceptions, also sounds remarkably similar to the type of articles we routinely write today. Husbands and wives should talk about their finances, the article advises, and make sure that both partners have wills and familiarity with the household assets and budgets. In fact, I wrote an article with very similar advice for our website not too long ago. With a few wording adjustments, I could have almost copied and pasted from the 1958 article. (The advertising, though, feels decidedly retro—"the world's first jet-prop airliner," telephones, and air-conditioning units populate the pages. A story on prices also gives away the decade: A physician's house call goes for just over $4 in Philadelphia, according to a chart, while a man's haircut is $1.50.)

A few pages later, the issue features a prominent woman stockbroker who is notably only identified by her late husband's name, "Mrs. Charles U. Bay." *U.S. News* asks her if she thinks the typical wife is prepared to handle the family finances in an emergency. "No, I don't think she is. That is particularly true of women in my generation—I am 57. The younger wife coming on is much more able than the middle-aged wife who has been more protected. I would say that the young people today are much more alive and knowledgeable. They haven't had all the care and protection that my age has had, and they know more of what it is all about."

Those "young women" of 1958 are today's grandmothers. I often hear women of that generation making similar observations:

That they might not be fully comfortably with earning and investing money, but they think and hope the younger generation is. Will today's young women—my daughter's generation—grow up to say the same thing? Or can we help them embrace a more equitable outlook?

We are fighting against some powerful factors: traditional gender roles, vested industry interests in male clients, and a dearth of women in the finance industry. But all three factors are changing as we speak. More women are breadwinners and in charge of their family's finances, financial companies are catering to their growing ranks of female clients, and more women are leading the industry.

As moms, there are several steps we can take to help our own sons and daughters build their financial futures: We can talk to them about money, especially our daughters. Tell them what you wish your twenty-five-year-old self knew. (When Allianz asked women what financial advice they would give to their daughters or granddaughters, the most common response was, "Don't depend on others for your financial security.") We can show our children that managing money is an essential life skill while modeling it for them. We can keep earning money, even in a reduced capacity, as we raise our children. Even the very traditional Mrs. Charles U. Bay quoted in the 1958 *U.S. News & World Report* article said women should at the very least be prepared to work, because at some point they might have to. We can use financial tools like estate planning documents and life insurance to protect ourselves so that if we or our partners are incapacitated, even temporarily, our finances will remain intact for our children.

We can also let our children inspire us and foster our commitment to our own financial security. I have never felt more ambitious as when I became a mom. Suddenly, I was no longer working so hard just for myself. It was about being able to provide for these new loves of my life.

While so much has changed in the world since that 1958 article was published, the way we talk about money hasn't caught up. Women are still too often reduced to shoppers and second-class investors when we're actually helming the decks of our family's financial well-being. So much rides on our decisions, including our children's futures.

Being a smart mom is also about so much more than money: It's about showing our children how to follow their dreams because they see us following ours, and about making daily choices that prioritize joy and happiness. I feel rich when I have the flexibility to leave work early to see a school performance or stay home with a sick child. When I spend a rainy afternoon watching a movie with my kids under a blanket while popovers bake in the oven. When I can take a half day off work to volunteer in my daughter's kindergarten classroom without worrying that it will negatively impact my job.

As one of my students later pointed out when I shared my daughter's comments about our pickup schedule, she might not really think that the money that comes from her dad's career takes precedence over her mom's. She was just concerned that her normal routine, which involves me picking her up from school, was being altered. She really just wants to know that someone she loves will be there for her—by far the most important thing that we parents provide. She probably doesn't really care who is putting money into the family bank account. But she certainly cares, even if she doesn't realize it, that there is enough money in there to pay for her food, home, clothes, and activities. And that responsibility increasingly falls to moms.

That's why these conversations matter—the financial security of our children depends on the choices that we make today.

SMART MOM
RICH MOM
HANDBOOK

The following templates, checklists, and to-do lists are designed to help you implement the ideas discussed throughout the book. The handbook features the following tools:

Family Money Goals

Financial Snapshot

Budget Planner

Purse Check: What to Ask Before You Buy

"Dear Daughter . . .": Sharing Your Money Lessons

What to Ask Your Parents

Financial Questions for Kids to Ask Grandparents

Legacy Checklist: Are You Prepared?

Smart Mom, Rich Mom Calendar: A Nine-Month
   Plan for Getting It Done

Mom Group Discussion Questions

• FAMILY MONEY GOALS •

The whole family can help fill out this worksheet, which is designed to spark a discussion about goals, priorities, and action steps.

How do we as a family define financial security?

_____

_____

_____

_____

Big family dreams (i.e., vacation, paying for college, retiring at age 50):

In the next year, we'd like to:

_____

_____

_____

_____

In the next five years, we'd like to:

_____

_____

_____

_____

In the next ten years and beyond, we'd like to:

_____

_____

_____

_____

Individual family member goals:

What can we spend less on today to help achieve these big goals? Are there areas where we feel we are wasting money? How can each family member contribute (i.e., turning off lights to save electricity, cooking the family dinner)?

_____

_____

_____

_____

What type of spending gives us the most enjoyment as a family? If we suddenly had an extra $1,000, how would we spend it?

_____

_____

_____

_____

As a family, how do we enjoy giving back to our community?

_____

_____

_____

_____

• FINANCIAL SNAPSHOT •

	ACCOUNT NAME	PASSWORD REMINDER	AMOUNT
NON-RETIREMENT ACCOUNTS:			
Checking account			
Savings account			
Brokerage account			
Other accounts			
RETIREMENT ACCOUNTS:			
401(k) account 1			
401(k) account 2			
401(k) account 3			
IRA account			
Other retirement accounts			
PHYSICAL ASSETS:			
Estimated home value			
Car			
LOANS AND DEBTS:			
Mortgage			
Student loans			
Credit card balance			
Other loans			
INSURANCE ACCOUNTS:			
Health			
Life			
Other			
Current net worth (subtract liabilities from assets):			

• BUDGET PLANNER •

MONTHLY HOUSEHOLD TAKE-HOME PAY (AFTER TAXES):	
MINUS RETIREMENT SAVINGS:	
SUBTRACT MONTHLY EXPENSES:	
Housing	
Food	
Transportation	
Child care	
Utilities	
Health care	
Other	
SUBTRACT MORE FLEXIBLE EXPENSES:	
Entertainment	
Kids' activities	
Eating out	
Professional expenses	
Personal care	
MONTHLY SAVINGS:	

• PURSE CHECK •
WHAT TO ASK BEFORE YOU BUY

The concept of asking yourself a series of questions before making purchases—often referred to as a "wallet buddy"—has been developed by organizations including the Center for a New American Dream and Jews United for Justice. Below, I customize the concept for moms. You can download an illustrated, wallet-size version from my website, kimberly-palmer.com, to keep in your purse as a reminder next time you pull out your credit card.

1. Will this product or service make my life easier in some way, or will it turn into one more thing that requires my time and energy?

2. Will I still be using it in a year?

3. Would I bring it with me if I had to move to a different home? Would I miss it if I didn't have it with me?

4. Will this purchase contribute to my long-term life goals? Will it create a meaningful family experience?

5. Are there ongoing monthly or annual costs associated with this purchase, including my time?

6. Does this product or service, and how it was made, reflect our family's values?

• "DEAR DAUGHTER . . ." •
SHARING YOUR MONEY LESSONS

What better way to impart your hard-won financial lessons to your children than by writing them a letter. No matter how many times you have showed them how to compare prices at the grocery store or encouraged them to save money for a rainy day, putting your thoughts into a letter lets them return to your wisdom whenever they want to. Here is a template that can be customized for your family.

Dear _____,

I am writing this letter to you today to share my financial lessons for you—the lessons that I hope I taught you as a child, but which can be hard to implement. I hope that you find it useful, especially when navigating the inevitable money challenges that you will face in your life.

    Let me start by telling you about a financial challenge of my own.

_____

_____

_____

_____

_____

_____

    One of the best money decisions that I made, which continues to contribute to our family's financial security today, was _____

_____.

Our choices have helped our family achieve _____

_____

and pay for _____

_____.

I encourage you to develop these financial habits as you get older:

1. _____

2. _____

3. _____

4. _____

5. _____

I hope that I can help you navigate your own money challenges and I look forward to watching as you find your financial footing. I hope this helps.

Love,
Mom xoxo

• WHAT TO ASK YOUR PARENTS •

Talking about money topics with your parents can lead to some heavy conversations. But they are ones that are important to have, both for your own financial security and that of your parents, and they only get harder with time if you wait to have them. Here are topics to consider discussing:

1. Have you saved enough money to support yourself in retirement? (You don't need to know all the details—just that they have sufficiently planned ahead to be solvent as they age.)
2. If you are unable to live alone, do you prefer to continue living at home with help, in a senior center, or with one of your children?
3. Where can I find information about your financial accounts, insurance policies, estate planning documents, and contact information for any relevant financial professionals? (Likewise, make sure you know how to shut down or otherwise manage your parents' social media accounts if they need you to.)
4. How do you want your money managed if you can no longer handle the task alone? (Your parents might want you, a sibling, or a financial professional to step in. If the task falls to you, then you'll want to read the free "Managing Someone Else's Money" guides on the website of the Consumer Financial Protection Bureau: cfpb.gov.)
5. How can I best help you? (Parents, as they age, often fear losing control, and you want to reassure them that you are available to assist, not take over. They are still in control of their money.)

• FINANCIAL QUESTIONS FOR KIDS •
TO ASK GRANDPARENTS

You don't have to do all the work. Grandparents and other older relatives have a big role to play, too, in how your kids learn to think about money. Encourage your kids to ask these kinds of questions of the older adults in their lives, adjusted to suit their ages:

1. Did you have any spending money when you were growing up, and if so, what did you spend it on?
2. What was your first job?
3. What's the biggest financial challenge you ever faced in your life?
4. When do you remember feeling richest?
5. When have you felt the poorest?
6. What's the best purchase you ever made?
7. How did you learn about money as a child?
8. What do you remember asking your parents to buy for you when you were growing up?
9. What's the biggest money mistake you think you made?
10. What do you wish you knew about money as a young adult?
11. How did you try to teach your own children about money?
12. What are your favorite frugal habits that help you save?

• LEGACY CHECKLIST •
ARE YOU PREPARED?

No one wants to think about life after we're gone, least of all mothers, but there are a few tasks to tackle before banishing the thought from your mind.

❑ Have you written a will that spells out your preferences for guardianship for your children as well as how you want your assets dispersed? Other essential documents include financial power of attorney, health care proxy (so someone else, like your partner, can make important health care decisions for you), and an overview of your financial documents, along with any relevant contact information (such as for a lawyer or financial adviser). If you've gone through any major life changes since last writing your will, including having more children, getting divorced or married, or acquiring significant assets, then you'll want to make updates.

❑ Do you have life insurance? You might have access to a life insurance policy through work, which you can supplement on the private market to reach the level of coverage that you desire. You'll want to consider how much money it would take to replace the income that you and your partner generate along with the expenses you would want the money to cover. A surviving parent might also want to cut back on work to be at home more with the children, and life insurance can help fund that choice, too.

❑ Is your beneficiary information up to date? On your retirement accounts and other financial accounts, you have the option to select a beneficiary. Make sure you update this information, especially if you've gotten married or divorced recently.

❑ Do you have disability insurance? If group disability insurance is available through your work or through professional associations, then it's usually a great deal that you'll want to take advantage of, in case you have to be temporarily out of the workforce because of an injury or illness. (You should also check on your partner's disability insurance status, too, and consider purchasing it for both of you if it is available through your workplace plans.)

❑ Are your digital assets prepared? Facebook offers the option of appointing someone to manage your account in the event of your death; other social media tools let you select privacy and security settings that will affect how your accounts are handled or deleted after death.

❑ Are all of your important documents, including wills, overview of financial accounts, Social Security number, and online passwords, in a place that will be accessible to those who need it in the event you are incapacitated?

• SMART MOM, RICH MOM CALENDAR •
A NINE-MONTH PLAN FOR GETTING IT DONE

If your financial to-do list feels overwhelming, the simplest approach is to break it down into smaller steps, so you can tackle just a handful of tasks each month and, by the end of one year, feel significantly more on top of your money. Here is a month-by-month guide to completing the action items outlined in the book:

MONTH 1

❑ Become a savvier shopper by using price comparison and coupon apps, such as RedLaser, RetailMeNot, and PriceGrabber. Before making online purchases, run a web search for the retailer's name and the word "coupon" and consider using a browser add-on such as PriceBlink or InvisibleHand so that you know you're getting the best deal.

❑ Try to repurpose or reuse items even after they are past their prime. Take a DIY approach around the house for easy repairs before calling in the professionals.

❑ Review your credit card statement carefully each month and check up on any charges you don't recognize; they can be the first sign of fraud or identity theft.

❑ Review the returns you are currently earning on your savings accounts. Keep short-term cash savings in FDIC-insured bank accounts and move longer-term savings that you don't need for at least five years into money market funds and other relatively conservative funds that pay a higher interest rate than the prevailing one on bank accounts. Target date funds will automatically shift the money into more conservative securities as you get closer to the date you need the funds.

❑ Pull your credit report at AnnualCreditReport.com and review it for any errors. If you find any, contact the credit bureau about removing the incorrect information. Improve your credit score over time by paying your bills on time.

MONTH 2

❑ Review your current spending patterns and savings rate. A free online tool like Mint.com can help identify overspending spots. To coordinate spending with a partner, consider an app like HomeBudget, which automatically syncs between phones.

❑ Identify your short- and long-term savings goals; write them down somewhere, in a planner or a calendar, where you'll be reminded of them weekly.

❑ Reflect on the older woman that you want to become. To connect with her, age your face using an aging app or website to see the future, older you; call an older woman in your family like your grandmother; or write a letter to your current self from your future self.

❑ Set aside time to review your current financial accounts and organize all of the related paperwork. Make a note of updates you need to make or paperwork you need to file. Repeat this process every three months.

MONTH 3

❏ Take a closer look at all child-related expenses, including child care, education, activities, food, and clothing. Consider whether there are ways to reduce the costs by trading hand-me-downs with friends or cooking more meals at home.

❏ Pick the more flexible parts of your budget to reduce—such as entertainment or clothing—and redirect the money into a savings account.

MONTH 4

❏ Assess your current career satisfaction and earning potential. Are there ways to grow your income without sacrificing more time away from your family? Perhaps you can consider pursuing more responsibility at work along with a telecommuting option, or launching some type of side business that you can work on from home.

❏ If you are currently taking a break from the workforce to care for your children, look for ways to continue contributing to your field or to keep your skills up to date. Getting involved with a professional organization, blogging on your LinkedIn profile, or attending networking events are possibilities.

❏ Review last year's tax paperwork to make sure you are maxing out all of the parenting-related tax benefits, including the child and dependent care credit. Likewise, continue to contribute to your retirement funds through an IRA, even during breaks from the workforce.

MONTH 5

❑ Ramp up your comfort with investing by reading websites like MarketWatch and Kiplinger. If you don't want the burden of regularly updating your investment choices, then consider a target date fund that will handle that job for you.

❑ Review your current investments and rebalance them to achieve your desired level of risk. Do this review at least once a year, and work with a fee-only financial adviser if you want customized guidance. Many retirement account providers offer free consults on your retirement investments; check with your workplace retirement account provider to see if this is an option for you.

❑ Talk with your partner to make sure you are on the same page when it comes to short- and long-term investments and that you each know where your money is and how it's being managed.

❑ Use an online retirement calculator (a quick web search brings up a handful, including the ones at Bankrate. com) to check that you are on track to reach your savings goals at your current rate of putting money away. Make any necessary adjustments by ramping up automatic contributions into your accounts.

❑ Open up 529 college savings accounts for your children and make a plan for regularly contributing money into the accounts each year.

MONTH 6

❑ Organize all of your household paperwork, including estate planning documents, big receipts, mortgage-related documents, and family paperwork such as birth certificates and marriage certificates. Store these items in a fireproof container that you can easily access when you need to. A digital storage system like FileThis can make it easier to stay on top of incoming paperwork.

❏ Review your social media accounts to make sure you are not oversharing details that could be used by thieves to log into your accounts. That includes birth dates, family names like your mother's maiden name, and even your wedding anniversary. At least once a year, review your privacy settings on Facebook and other social media accounts because they are constantly being updated and the default might share more information with strangers than you intend.

❏ Ask yourself if you are prepared financially to manage money on your own, should you suddenly need to do so. If not, get ready by talking to your partner more about your finances and making sure you are familiar with your accounts and financial strategy.

MONTH 7

❏ Talk with your parents about their plans and preferences for growing older. How can you best help them prepare for any challenges that come up as they age? Is their paperwork in order, and do you know where to find important documents if needed, such as their health care preferences? Schedule an in-depth chat with your parents so that you are prepared in case a health crisis hits.

❏ Involve any siblings in a discussion of how you will handle any care that your parents need as they age. If you are sharing duties, look for ways to balance the responsibility evenly.

❑ If you are concerned about the cognitive decline of aging parents or the risk of their making financial mistakes (or becoming victim to fraud), check with your parents' bank about adding additional monitoring to their accounts, so you are notified of large withdrawals, for example.

MONTH 8

❑ Reflect on the financial habits you are currently demonstrating for your children. Do they see you making spending decisions and are there ways you can involve them more in the process, such as when comparison shopping? Can they watch as you pay the monthly household bills? Can a discussion of family values and priorities come up naturally around the dinner table, when discussing vacation plans?

❑ Encourage your children to ask your parents about their own financial experiences growing up. Were there hard times that your parents can share? By imparting such information they are helping to pass down family history and helping your children learn about the value of a dollar.

❑ Create an allowance system that works for your family based on the age of your children and what types of expenses you want them to handle. Starting around age five, they're ready to begin saving money for purchases that they want.

MONTH 9

❑ Flesh out your own big dreams and plans as your children grow more independent. Do you want to launch a business? Consider buying the domain name and getting started now. Do you want to shift careers, update your skills with a new degree or certification, or revamp your online presence to tap into a new community? Invest in yourself.

❑ As your children grow, encourage them to become more financially independent, too. Help them set up their first budget and open a retirement account when they start their first job. In this way you are also helping them figure out their adult lives.

These questions are designed as discussion starters for moms' groups, including book clubs, playdate groups, and coffee dates. Talking about money with friends can be awkward, yes, but it can also lead to supportive conversations and, ultimately, smarter money choices. These questions help you talk through some of the concepts in the book (identified by chapter) with the goal of minimizing any discomfort and maximizing the benefits. (You can get a version to download and print out for your group at kimberly-palmer.com.)

1. In the introduction, we learn about the disparity in financial literacy between even young girls and boys. Have you noticed this already with your own children or friends, or did you notice it growing up? What do you think explains it, and what can be done to mitigate it? What do you want your children to know about money as they get older, and how do you plan to teach it to them?

2. How would you characterize the interactions you've had with the financial services industry, whether taking out insurance, working with a financial adviser, or opening up a retirement account at work?

3. Who controls the finances in your household, including spending, bill paying, and managing tasks related to insurance and savings? Do you like the current division of responsibilities or are there aspects about it you want to change?

4. After reading *Smart Mom, Rich Mom,* are there steps you want to take to improve your own

financial security? Some of the action steps we've
mentioned include taking out life insurance (for
both yourself and your partner), starting to save for
your children's college expenses through a 529
account, or talking to your own parents about their
future and any help they might need from you.

5. In Chapter 2, we learn how useful it can be to
articulate short- and long-term financial goals for
yourself and your family, as a first step toward
taking the action required to achieve them. What
are your short- and long-term goals, and do you
already have ideas for how you plan to make them
happen?

6. Another exercise we learn about in Chapter 2
involves imagining your future self, since research
shows that doing so can help inspire us to save
more money today for taking care of ourselves
tomorrow. What do you think your eighty-year-old
self would say to your current self when it comes to
your finances?

7. In Chapter 4, we learn that many moms pursue
nonlinear career paths, especially as they juggle
their schedules to care for children. Are there
aspects of your current work situation that you
would like to shift, whether it's pursuing more
flexibility, higher pay, different hours, or an
alternate career altogether?

8. Are there areas of your spending that you know
you want to cut back on so that you can use that
money for something else, like savings? Or have
you discovered any creative ways to save money
while still managing all your household expenses?

9. Do you currently use an allowance system in your

home to help teach your children the value of money, and if so, how does it work for you? Do you express to your children your own thoughts on managing money in different ways, through example or conversation?

10. If you are not there yet (and even if it's a long way off), how do you imagine your retirement years unfolding? Will you live somewhere else? Will you try something new like volunteer work or travel? Are you taking any steps now, like putting money into a retirement account, to prepare for that day?

• NOTES •

INTRODUCTION: INTO MOTHERHOOD

2   *According to Fidelity . . .*

"Are Women Standing Up to the Retirement Savings Challenge?" 2013, Fidelity, communications.fidelity.com/wi/2013/womeninvesting/assets/ women_in_investing_whitepaper.pdf.

2   *The Pew Research Center . . .*

Wendy Wang, Kim Parker, and Paul Taylor, "Breadwinner Moms," Pew Research Center, May 29, 2013, www.pewsocialtrends.org/2013/05/29/ breadwinner-moms/.

2   *Similarly, the rise of blended families . . .*

Jens Manual Krogstad, "5 Facts About the Modern American Family," April 30, 2014, www.pewresearch.org/fact-tank/2014/04/30/5-facts-about-the -modern-american-family/.

2   *A report from the Boston Consulting Group . . .*

Michael J. Silverstein and Katherine Sayre, "Women Want More: A Revolutionary Opportunity," Boston Consulting Group, September 9, 2009, www. bcgperspectives.com/content/articles/consumer_products_marketing_sales _women_want_more_excerpt/.

3   *70 percent of women promptly replace . . .*

Heather R. Ettinger and Eileen M. O'Connor, "Women of Wealth," Family Wealth Advisors Council, 2013, hemingtonwm.com/wp-content/ uploads/2013/11/FWAC_WomenOfWealth.pdf; see also "The Allianz Women, Money, and Power Study, 2013," www2.allianzlife.com/content/ public/Literature/Documents/Modern_Family.pdf.

3   *At one event held on Capitol Hill . . .*

Kimberly Palmer, "Why Millennial Women Have a Money Problem," June 17, 2014, USNews.com, money.usnews.com/money/blogs/alpha-consumer

/2014/06/17/why-millennial-women-have-a-money-problem; see also "PISA 2012 Results," http://www.oecd.org/pisa/keyfindings/pisa-2012 -results.htm.

6   *A 2014 T. Rowe Price survey . . .*

Kimberly Palmer, "Why Boys Know More About Money," August 22, 2014, USNews.com, money.usnews.com/money/blogs/alpha-consumer/ 2014/08/22/why-boys-know-more-about-money.

6   *A 2015 Fidelity survey . . .*

Kimberly Palmer, "How Women Can Boost Their Financial Confidence," March 4, 2015, USNews.com, money.usnews.com/money/personal-finance/articles/ 2015/03/04/how-women-can-boost-their-financial-confidence.

6   *Elizabeth Warren's research . . .*

Elizabeth Warren and Amelia Warren Tyagi, *The Two-Income Trap* (New York: Basic Books, 2003), 6.

CHAPTER ONE: SAVE (AND SPEND) LIKE A MOTHER

13   *A 2014 Wells Fargo survey found . . . "*

"Wells Fargo Survey: Affluent Women 'Enjoy' Making Money," November 20, 2014, Wells Fargo, www.wellsfargo.com/about/press/2014/affluent -woman-making-money_112/.

16   *"She would cut the Guess patch off a pair of jeans . . ."*

Kimberly Palmer, "The Truth About Growing Up 'American Middle Class'" USNews.com, November 19, 2014, money.usnews.com/money/blogs/alpha -consumer/2014/11/19/the-truth-about-growing-up-american-middle -class.

CHAPTER TWO: OWNING IT

39   *Researchers at the University at Buffalo Jacobs School of Medicine and Biomedical Sciences . . .*

Roberto Ferdman, "The Stark Difference Between What Poor Babies and Rich Babies Eat," November 4, 2014, *Washington Post*, www.washingtonpost .com/blogs/wonkblog/wp/2014/11/04/the-stark-difference-between-what -poor-babies-and-rich-babies-eat/.

39   *the bank HSBC . . .*

"New HSBC Direct 'ASK' Survey Shows Active Savers Better Prepared to Weather the Storm," May 29, 2009, HSBC.

NOTES

39   *Back before you were a mom . . .*

"Table 3. Age of Reference Person: Average Annual Expenditures and Characteristics, Consumer Expenditure Survey, 2011," www.bls.gov/cex/2011/Standard/age.pdf.

39   *According to a 2015 Financial Finesse report . . .*

"2015 Financial Stress Report, Executive Summary," Financial Finesse, June 2015. www.financialfinesse.com/wp-content/uploads/2015/06/Financial-Stress-Report_2015.pdf.

40   *The U.S. Department of Agriculture estimates . . .*

Mark Lino (2014). "Expenditures on Children by Families, 2013." U.S. Department of Agriculture, Center for Nutrition Policy and Promotion. Miscellaneous Publication No. 1528-2013, www.cnpp.usda.gov/sites/default/files/expenditures_on_children_by_families/crc2013.pdf.

40   *According to research by Hal Hershfield . . .*

Kimberly Palmer, "How to Meet Your Future Self—and Save," February 13, 2012, USNews.com, money.usnews.com/money/blogs/alpha-consumer/2012/02/13/how-to-meet-your-future-selfand-save.

42   *The Center for Retirement Research at Boston College . . .*

Alicia Munnell, Anthony Webb, and Francesca N. Golub-Sass, "How Much to Save for a Secure Retirement," November 2011, crr.bc.edu/briefs/how-much-to-save-for-a-secure-retirement/.

43   *Research based on the spending patterns of 2,500 households . . .*

Kimberly Palmer, "Americans Spend Less When They Fear Layoffs," July 16, 2014, USNews.com, money.usnews.com/money/blogs/alpha-consumer/2014/07/16/americans-spend-less-when-they-fear-layoffs.

44   *Women are actually more likely than men . . .*

Kimberly Palmer, "BMO Harris Bank Survey Shows Better Credit Card Behavior Among Men Than Women," October 28, 2014, BMO Harris, newsroom.bmoharris.com/press-releases/bmo-harris-bank-survey-shows-better-credit-card-be-1154337.

48   *a 2014 study from UBS Wealth Management . . .*

Kimberly Palmer, "Couples Are Happier Sharing Money Decisions," May 9, 2014, USNews.com, money.usnews.com/money/blogs/alpha-consumer/2014/05/09/couples-are-happier-sharing-money-decisions.

NOTES

CHAPTER THREE: TIMING IS EVERYTHING

51   *Babies born today . . .*

Mark Lino, (2014). "Expenditures on Children by Families," 2013. U.S. Department of Agriculture, Center for Nutrition Policy and Promotion. Miscellaneous Publication No. 1528-2013, www.cnpp.usda.gov/sites/default/files/expenditures_on_children_by_families/cre2013.pdf.

51   *For many women, the costliest part of having babies . . .*

Michelle J. Budig and Paula England, "The Wage Penalty for Motherhood," *American Sociological Review*, Volume 66, pp. 204–225, April 2001. www.asanet.org/images/members/docs/pdf/featured/motherwage.pdf.

52   *Research shows that in general . . .*

Amalia R. Miller, "The Effects of Motherhood Timing on Career Path," *Journal of Population Economics*, Volume 24, Issue 3, pp. 1071–1100, July 2011, link.springer.com/article/10.1007%2Fs00148-009-0296-x.

57   *When the Pew Research Center asked prospective parents . . .*

"Young, Underemployed and Optimistic," February 2, 2012, Pew Research Center, www.pewsocialtrends.org/2012/02/09/young-underemployed-and-optimistic/.

CHAPTER FOUR: LIKE A BOSS

64   *Farnoosh Torabi, a money expert and TV personality . . .*

Farnoosh Torabi, "Mommyhood Musings: The Baby Effect and My New Business Idea," October 21, 2014, Farnoosh.tv, farnoosh.tv/mommyhood-musings-baby-effect-new-business-idea/.

67   *On one high-powered panel, Bob Moritz . . .*

White House Summit on Working Families, June 23, 2014, workingfamiliessummit.org/.

66   *According to research conducted at the University of Rhode Island . . .*

Kimberly Palmer, "The Cost of Caring for Aging Parents," August 27, 2014, USNews.com, money.usnews.com/money/personal-finance/articles/2014/08/27/the-cost-of-caring-for-aging-parents; see also Kenneth Matos and Ellen Galinksy, "2014 National Study of Employers," 2014, familiesandwork.org/downloads/2014NationalStudyOfEmployers.pdf.

73   *Pamela Stone, professor of sociology at Hunter College . . .*

NOTES

Kimberly Palmer, "The Real Cost of Women Opting Out," July 30, 2014, USNews.com, money.usnews.com/money/personal-finance/articles/2014/07/30/the-real-cost-of-women-opting-out.

74   *The kaleidoscope career . . .*

Lisa Mainiero and Sherry Sullivan, *The Opt-Out Revolt: Why People Are Leaving Companies to Create Kaleidoscope Careers* (Mountain View, CA: Davies-Black Publishing, 2006).

74   *Jamie Ladge, a professor at Northeastern University . . .*

Kimberly Palmer, "The Real Impact of Babies on Career Success," September 16, 2011, USNews.com, money.usnews.com/money/blogs/alpha-consumer/2011/09/16/the-real-impact-of-babies-on-career-success.

76   *In her PhD research at Purdue University, Elizabeth Wilhoit . . .*

Elizabeth Wilhoit, "Opting Out (Without Kids): Understanding Non-Mothers' Workplace Exit in Popular Autobiographies," September 25, 2013, *Gender Work & Organization*, Volume 21, Issue 3, p. 260–272, May 2014, onlinelibrary.wiley.com/doi/10.1111/gwao.12034/abstract.

CHAPTER FIVE: INVESTING MAMAS

88   *In a study on couples and retirement investments . . .*

"2013 Couples Retirement Study Executive Summary," Fidelity Investments, 2013, www.fidelity.com/static/dcle/welcome/documents/CouplesRetirementStudy.pdf.

89   *A 2014 Wells Fargo survey of over 1,800 women . . .*

"Wells Fargo Survey: Affluent Women 'Enjoy' Making Money," November 20, 2014, Wells Fargo, www.wellsfargo.com/about/press/2014/affluent-woman-making-money_112/.

91   *According to the Transamerica Center for Retirement Studies . . .*

"Fourteen Facts About Women's Retirement Outlook," March 2014, Transamerica Center for Retirement Studies, www.transamericacenter.org/docs/default-source/resources/women-and-retirement/tcrs2014_report_women_and_retirement_14_facts.pdf

91   *the latest government statistics show . . .*

"Retirement Security: Women Still Face Challenges," United States Government Accountability Office, Report to the Chairman, Special Committee on Aging, U.S. Senate, July 2012, www.gao.gov/assets/600/592726.pdf.

NOTES

94   *In fact, the Center's analysis shows that if you start saving at age 25 . . .*

Alicia Munnell, Anthony Webb, and Francesca N. Golub-Sass, "How Much to Save for a Secure Retirement," November 2011, crr.bc.edu/briefs/how-much-to-save-for-a-secure-retirement/.

97   *A Fidelity white paper on women and investing . . .*

"Are Women Standing Up to the Retirement Savings Challenge?" 2013, Fidelity, communications.fidelity.com/wi/2013/womeninvesting/assets/women_in_investing_whitepaper.pdf.

99   *According to research by Judy Postmus . . .*

Judy Postmus, Andrea Hetling, and Gretchen L. Hoge, "Evaluating a Financial Education Curriculum as an Intervention to Improve Financial Behaviors and Financial Well-Being of Survivors of Domestic Violence," December 30, 2014, *Journal of Consumer Affairs*, Volume 49, Issue 1, p. 250–266, Spring 2015, onlinelibrary.wiley.com/doi/10.1111/joca.12057/abstract.

102   *A 2014 survey by Allianz found that among single parents . . .*

"College Savings Take Priority for Today's Single Parents," August 4, 2014, Allianz LoveFamilyMoney Study, www.allianzlife.com/about/news-and-events/news-releases/Press-Release-August-4-2014.

103   *An analysis done by Vanguard for the* New York Times *shows . . .*

Ron Lieber, "Taxing 529 College Savings Plans: A Plan That Went Awry," January 30, 2015, *New York Times*, www.nytimes.com/2015/01/31/your-money/paying-for-college/the-wouldve-shouldve-and-couldve-of-taxing-529-plans.html?_r=0.

CHAPTER SIX: PLAYING DEFENSE

111   *The U.S. Census Bureau reports that for those between the ages of 40 and 44 . . .*

"Marriage and Divorce: Patterns by Gender, Race, and Educational Attainment," October 2013, Monthly Labor Review, U.S. Bureau of Labor Statistics, www.bls.gov/opub/mlr/2013/article/pdf/marriage-and-divorce-patterns-by-gender-race-and-educational-attainment.pdf.

119   *The Hartford Financial Services Group reports that fewer than half of workers in their twenties and early thirties . . .*

"The Hartford Gets 'Social' to Help Gen Y Maximize Benefits, Take Control of Career," October 2, 2012, The Hartford, newsroom.thehartford.com/releases/the-hartford-gets-social-to-help-gen-y-maximize-benefits-take-control-of-career.

NOTES

121   *According to a 2014 New York Life survey . . .*

"Widows Under Stress: Widows Confront Years of Undue Hardship After the Loss of a Spouse, a New Study Reveals," November 17, 2014, New York Life, www.newyorklife.com/about/widows-under-stress.

CHAPTER SEVEN: STUCK IN THE MIDDLE

132   *The Family Wealth Advisors Council, a network of fee-only wealth management firms, found that . . .*

Heather R. Ettinger and Eileen M. O'Connor, "Women of Wealth," Family Wealth Advisors Council, 2013, familywealthadvisorscouncil.com/sandwich -generation-woman/.

132   *The MetLife Study of Caregiving Costs to Working Caregivers . . .*

"Caregiving Costs Americans $3 Trillion in Lost Wages, Pension and Social Security Benefits," June 14, 2011, MetLife Mature Market Institute, www.metlife .com/assets/cao/mmi/publications/mmi-pressroom/2011/mmi-caregiving -costs-working-caregivers-pr.pdf.

133   *According to Census Bureau data analyzed by the UCLA Center for Health Policy Research . . .*

Steven P. Wallace, "The Graying of the Rainbow," talk presented at the 2014 Gerontology Society of America Conference, Washington, D.C.

135   *A 2014 survey of 1,345 family caregivers by Caring.com . . .*

"Nearly Half of Family Caregivers Spend Over $5,000 per Year on Caregiving Costs," September 15, 2015, Caring.com, www.caring.com/about/ news-room/costs-of-caregiving-2014.

138   *The 2014 Fidelity Intra-Family Generational Finance Study . . .*

"Fidelity's 2014 Intra-Family Generational Finance Study Executive Summary," 2014, Fidelity, www.fidelity.com/bin-public/060_www_fidelity _com/documents/fidelity/2014-intra-family-generational-study.pdf.

141   *According to a survey of 1,000 adults by Caring.com . . .*

"Living Trust and Wills When Caring for Elderly Parents," 2015, Caring. com, www.caring.com/research/wills-data-2015.

CHAPTER EIGHT: MODEL MOMS

147   *a study came out from T. Rowe Price . . .*

NOTES

"Boys and Girls Not Equally Prepared for Financial Futures," August 18, 2014, T. Rowe Price, corporate.troweprice.com/Money-Confident-Kids/ Site/Media/News/Articles/boys-and-girls-not-equally-prepared-for -financial-future.

147   *A 2011 Charles Schwab survey of teens . . .*

"2011 Teens & Money Survey Findings," 2011, Charles Schwab, www .schwabmoneywise.com/public/file/P-4192268/110526-SCHWAB -TEENSMONEY.pdf.

155   *The nonprofit Common Sense Media has found . . .*

"Advertising to Children and Teens: Current Practices," January 28, 2014, Common Sense Media, www.commonsensemedia.org/research/advertising -to-children-and-teens-current-practices.

155   *A study from University of Arizona found . . .*

Paul M. Connell, Merrie Brucks, and Jesper H. Nielsen, "How Childhood Advertising Exposure Can Create Biased Product Evaluations That Persist into Adulthood," January 9, 2014, *Journal of Consumer Research*, www .jcr-admin.org/files/pressPDFs/030614095007_March2014.pdf.

160   *Research by Linda Babcock and Sara Laschever . . .*

Linda Babcock and Sara Laschever, "Women Don't Ask: Negotiation and the Gender Divide," www.womendontask.com/stats.html.

161   *In a 2014 TIAA-CREF survey of over 1,000 grandchildren . . .*

"Only 8 Percent of Grandparents Are Likely to Talk with Grandchildren about Money and Saving for College," August 5, 2014, TIAA-CREF, www.tiaa-cref .org/public/about/press/about_us/releases/articles/pressrelease512.html.

163   *And most parents—70 percent, according to a 2015 T. Rowe Price survey . . .*

"T. Rowe Price: Parents Let Kids Learn About Money the Hard Way," March 25, 2015, T. Rowe Price, corporate.troweprice.com/Money-Confident-Kids/ Site/Media/News/Articles/trp-parents-let-kids-learn-about-money-the -hard-way.

CHAPTER NINE: BACK TO YOU

181   *According to the Pew Research Center's Internet and American Life Project . . .*

Keith Hampton, Lee Rainie, Weixu Lu, Inyoung Shin, and Kristen Purcell, "Social Media and the Cost of Caring," January 15, 2015, Pew Research Center, www.pewinternet.org/2015/01/15/social-media-and-stress/.

NOTES

CHAPTER TEN: RETURNING TO THE NEST

176 *A 2012 Charles Schwab survey found that one in three middle-income workers in their sixties . . .*

"Charles Schwab's Older Workers & Money Survey Reveals Surprising Findings About Job Sentiment Among Americans in Their 50s and 60s," April 24, 2012, Charles Schwab, pressroom.aboutschwab.com/press-release/corporate-and-financial-news/charles-schwabs-older-workers-money-survey-reveals-surpri.

187 *The Social Security Administration publishes a great booklet . . .*

"What Every Woman Should Know," Social Security Administration, www.ssa.gov/pubs/EN-05-10127.pdf.

189 *In fact, a 2015 report from the Pew Research Center . . .*

Richard Fry, "More Millennials Living with Family Despite Improved Job Market," July 29, 2015, Pew Research Center, www.pewsocialtrends.org/2015/07/29/more-millennials-living-with-family-despite-improved-job-market/.

192 *According to TD Ameritrade's 2015 Financial Disruptions survey . . .*

"Financial Disruptions Survey, Impact of Life Events 2015," 2015, TD Ameritrade, www.amtd.com/files/doc_downloads/research/Disruptor_Survey_2015.pdf.

EPILOGUE: MORE THAN MONEY

202 *When Allianz asked women . . .*

"Meet Today's Modern Family," The Allianz Women, Money and Power Study, 2013, www2.allianzlife.com/content/public/Literature/Documents/Modern_Family.pdf.

• INDEX •

INDEX

INDEX

INDEX

INDEX

INDEX

INDEX

• ABOUT THE AUTHOR •

Kimberly Palmer is the author of *The Economy of You: Discover Your Inner Entrepreneur and Recession-Proof Your Life* and was the senior money editor at *US News & World Report* for nine years. She is also an adjunct professor at American University, where she teaches a course on mastering social media. She lives with her family, including two children, in the Washington, D.C., area. You can find her at kimberly-palmer.com.